THE MAKING OF *CITIZEN KANE*

5

The Making
of
Citizen Kane

Robert L. Carringer

John Murray

for Sonia

First published in Great Britain 1985 by
John Murray (Publishers) Ltd
50 Albemarle Street, London wix 4BD

© 1985 by The Regents of the University of California

Printed in Great Britain
at The Camelot Press, Southampton

British Library CIP Data
Carringer, Robert L.
The making of Citizen Kane.
1. Citizen Kane (Motion picture)
I. Title
791.43'72   PN1997.C/
ISBN 0-7195-4248-0

Contents

Preface

"It is, above all, the creation of one man."[1] That pronouncement on *Citizen Kane* by an early critic set the terms on which discussion of the film would be centered for decades to come. The quotation could serve as an epigraph to the auteur movement in film criticism. According to the auteur approach, the director is the real author of a film, and films should be regarded primarily as expressions of directorial intent. *Citizen Kane* was for critics the centerpiece of this movement. As a visually iconoclastic and resolutely individualistic work made in the Hollywood studio system but despite it, Welles's film seemed to represent a kind of ultimate vindication of the auteur premise. Pauline Kael's well-publicized case on behalf of *Citizen Kane* screenwriter Herman Mankiewicz forced acknowledgment of his important contribution, but for the most part it only served to stiffen auteurist recalcitrance to issues of collaboration.[2] When film entered the university in the 1970s, the single-author approach was the most popular one, especially in literature departments. Once again, *Citizen Kane* occupied the center of discussion. According to surveys, it was far and away the film most often studied in college and university film classes. James Naremore's *The Magic World of Orson Welles*, the first certifiably academic book on its subject, made what had become a familiar claim: "*Citizen Kane* is the product of an individual artist (and a company of his associates) working at a particular movie studio at a particular historical moment."[3] In contrast, this study attempts to show that the collaborative process provides the best framework for understanding the remarkable achievement this film represents.

By *collaborative process* I mean the sharing of the creative function by the director with others. A collaborator, in the most general sense of the term, is anyone who makes a distinguishable contribution to a film — from the writer or cinematographer down through the ranks to the wardrobe manager and casting director and even the still photographer assigned to the set. By studio custom, those making the most significant contributions to a film were identified by name and title in a credit sequence at the beginning. Most commonly, these were the producer, the players, the key technical and crafts personnel, the writer, and the director. (In practice, appearance in the screen credits was sometimes a privilege of rank. As we shall see, screen credits are not always a reliable guide to the nature or extent of an individual contribution.) The collaborators who concern me here form a subgroup within the credit list: the technical and crafts specialists who are in charge of a film's architectonics. The most important in the production phase are the screenwriter, the art director, and the cinematographer. Together, they are chiefly responsible for the conception, design, construction, and mechanical implementation of the facsimile spaces that are the camera's subject. (Scripts are usually thought of strictly in literary terms. Actually, a script is also an original working plan of the film's physical requirements.) Most important in the postproduction phase, when certain operations are performed on the footage and sound track derived in shooting, are the special effects technicians, the sound engineers, the music director, and the editor. Collectively, these two groups are the principal managers of a film's resources. Their charge is to deliver the highest technical quality and aesthetic values achievable at a designated price. Whatever the creative circumstances, it was in Welles's nature as an artist to make the most extravagant demands. Also, in most filmmaking matters he was an amateur. For these reasons, it was especially crucial for him to have the best talent in these key positions. In the making of *Citizen Kane*, he was fortunate to have collaborators who were well qualified, in some instances gifted, and in a few cases truly inspired. *Citizen Kane* is not only Hollywood's greatest film, but it is also, I contend, Hollywood's single most successful instance of collaboration. In a very real sense, the two propositions are synonymous.

This study is in the form of an extended chronological history of the production. The chapters correspond to the main phases in the making of a feature film — scripting, art direction, principal photography, and postproduction. In each chapter, I identify the key individuals involved, describe their functions, characterize their working relationship with Welles, and delineate the nature and extent of their individual contributions. The circumstances of collaboration are also instrumental, I think, in the fate of two other of Welles's efforts of the time — the adaptation of Conrad's *Heart of Darkness* that he intended to make before *Citizen Kane;* and *The Magnificent Ambersons,* his next film after it. The first and last chapters are abbreviated histories of these two productions that illustrate the theme.

A Word on Sources

The production history of *Citizen Kane* has been a favorite subject of film writing. The first attempt at a comprehensive treatment was by Roy Fowler in his 1946 biography of Welles. Fowler's account was based largely on film industry trade publications, which are extremely unreliable (see *Time,* September 27, 1982, p. 50, for an explanation), but it remained the accepted version until Charles Higham's *The Films of Orson Welles* (1970). Higham reworked the trade press material, researched other printed sources, interviewed several witnesses and participants in the film's making, and was granted access to the Mercury Theatre files. He did not always adequately verify his factual information, but Higham's account is still the best general overview of the film's history.[4] Ronald Gottesman reprinted contemporary reviews and several other valuable documents from the time (including pieces by Welles, Bernard Herrmann, and Gregg Toland) in *Focus on "Citizen Kane"* (1971). Pauline Kael was notoriously onesided in her treatment of the scripting history (see Chapter Two), but "Raising Kane" (1971) added extremely valuable new information from such interview subjects as George Schaefer and Robert Wise. Peter Bogdanovich gave Welles's answer to Kael and provided new evidence from the Mercury files in "The Kane Mutiny" (1972).[5] Joseph McBride contributed new information from his interviews with Welles and Welles associates in *Orson Welles* (1972).[6] One important piece of work was, unfortunately, never published — Donald W. Rea's 1966 master's thesis, which is especially valuable for its interview material and technical information.[7]

The foundation for the present work is a major resource not previously accessible, the Welles Collection in the archives of RKO Pictures, Los Angeles. This collection contains the production records, correspondence, and script, personnel, and legal files for all Welles's RKO projects, including those not produced or released. For *Citizen Kane,* there are also files on editing, music, screen and advertising credits, publicity, exhibition, Hearst, and the copyright infringement case brought by Ferdinand Lundberg (see Chapter Two), plus a set of early art department sketches. I have also made use of the Mercury Theatre Collection — first thanks to the kindness of Richard Wilson when it was still in his possession, later at Lilly Library, Indiana University, Bloomington. The RKO and Mercury Theatre collections substantially duplicate each other, but some types of materials are found only in the RKO files (for instance, on policy matters involving the Welles unit, as opposed to direct dealings with it), while others are found only in the Mercury files (for instance, on Mercury's internal operations, on Welles's dealings with others outside RKO, and preliminary script and production documents that never became part of the official production process). For purposes of citation, the master collection is the RKO file, designated *RKO* in the notes. Unique items in the Mercury Theatre Collection are designated *Mercury*. If there is no designation, it may be assumed that the item is in the RKO file.

Much of my technical information is derived from original interviews with professionals who were associated with the making of the film; in several cases, such as sound and art direction, they checked my preliminary drafts for technical accuracy. I had several long discussions with Welles himself. He also read and commented on Chapter Four, which has been published as an article. At his suggestion, I have introduced information he gave me with "Welles says" or "Welles told me" rather than "According to Welles," which he thought too formal in tone.

Much of the factual information that appears in this book is new. If something at variance with earlier accounts is presented here without specific documentation, it is based on the production records, or it has been independently verified.

Acknowledgments

I would first like to thank Orson Welles for talking with me at length about *Citizen Kane*. Richard Wilson, film director and longtime Welles associate, granted me access to the Mercury Theatre files and helped to open other doors. An enlightened administration at RKO General made this book possible, in particular Shane O'Neil, president, and Bette LeVine, business manager for RKO Pictures. Several former RKO employees who were involved in the making of *Citizen Kane* supplied background information and materials from their private files: Hilyard Brown, Linwood Dunn, Amalia Kent, John Mansbridge, Maurice Seiderman, Darrell Silvera, James G. Stewart, Robert Wise, and Maurice Zuberano. Vernon Harbin, archivist emeritus of RKO Pictures, Los Angeles, gave me expert guidance through the studio's history and rescued me from a premature interpretation more than once.

As always, it is a pleasure to thank certain professionals and their organizations and institutions for services generously performed: Sam Gill and Tony Slide, Academy of Motion Picture Arts and Sciences; Marc Wanamaker, Bison Film Archives; Kellam DeForest, DeForest Research; Saundra Taylor, Lilly Library; Emily Sieger, Motion Picture Section, Library of Congress; Charles Silver, Film Study Center, Museum of Modern Art; Elaine Felsher, Time, Inc. Archives; Robert Rosen, UCLA Film Archive; Audree Malkin, Theater Arts Library, UCLA; and Robert Knutson, Cinema Library, University of Southern California. Colleagues at the University of Illinois at Urbana–Champaign assisted in numerous ways, especially Edwin Jahiel, director, and Richard Leskosky, assistant director, Unit for Cinema Studies; Walter Creese, professor of architecture; and reference librarians Connie Fairchild, Carol Penka, and Dick Smith.

Others who helped include Nancy Allen, Dudley Andrew, Richard Betts, David Bradley, Frank Brady, Mike Briggs, Greg Brull, Kevin Cain, David Chierichetti, Michael Collins, Joseph Cotten, Alexander Doty, Allen Estrin, Regina Fadiman, Chris Fiscus, Richard France, Norman Gambill, David Gerrick, Ron Gottesman, Ron Haver, Charles Higham, Steven P. Hill, Ralph Hoge, John Houseman, George Jenkins, Richard Jewell, Kathryn Kalinak, Bruce Kawin, Vance Kepley, Jr., Maureen Kiernan,

Chuck McCaffrey, Fergus MacIvor, Charles Maland, Sara Mankiewicz, James Naremore, James Palmer, Barry Sabath, George Scheetz, Paul Stewart, Robert Tallman, Rene Wahlfeldt, Delores Wallace, and Betty Wilson.

The Campus Research Board, Graduate College, University of Illinois, provided an assistant, travel funds, and other forms of financial support. The manuscript was completed during an appointment in the Center for Advanced Study, University of Illinois.

Finally, I am deeply grateful to John Hall of RKO for his enthusiasm and total commitment to the book.

1

Heart of Darkness

Given Welles's ambitions and the continually perilous state of his finances, he was almost certain to end up in Hollywood sooner or later. That he was able to make the move on such favorable terms was the doing of RKO studio head George J. Schaefer. Schaefer lured Welles to Hollywood with a contract that guaranteed him a degree of artistic control virtually unheard of in the industry. (Considering Welles's lack of experience, the arrangement is all the more astonishing.) Welles was engaged to produce, direct, write, and act in two feature films. Their completion deadlines were scheduled so that he could have time off for other projects in between. RKO had to approve the story selected and also the budget, if it exceeded $500,000. Beyond that, Welles was to be allowed to work without interference, developing the story as he saw fit, engaging his own talent — not just performers but creative and technical personnel as well — and, most significantly, editing the final product his own way. Schaefer approached Welles at just the right time. His ambitious *Five Kings* Shakespeare production with John Houseman for the Theatre Guild had been forced to close in Philadelphia in the spring of 1939 without coming to New York. The Mercury Theatre stage operation had been shut down since the resounding flop of *Danton's Death* the previous fall. The RKO contract was not only a tremendous personal opportunity for Welles, but it held out the prospect of revitalizing the Mercury, expanding its horizons, and, quite possibly, of serving as a springboard for its return to Broadway. Welles and Houseman, as copartners in the Mercury, made the trip West together and signed the RKO contract on July 21, 1939.[1]

Schaefer's actions have been interpreted as everything from a move by a Nelson Rockefeller–led cabal in the parent company to an act of desperation brought on by the studio's financial plight. Actually, as Richard Jewell has shown in a carefully documented study, not only was RKO in a brief period of relative financial sanguinity at the time, but the signing of Welles was a logical development in a corporate policy that Schaefer had instituted.[2] When he took over as studio head in 1938, RKO was known for the Rogers–Astaire musicals, solid but modest dialogue comedies and melodramas, an occasional action adventure or spectacular, and a great deal of merely routine program filler. Schaefer set out to add a more artistically prestigious component to the studio's product line by making a series of independent production deals involving quality talent and literary properties. He signed contracts with, among others, Max Gordon's Broadway production syndicate, the screenwriting team of Gene Towne and Graham Baker, British producer Herbert Wilcox, and, later, Gabriel Pascal (who controlled the rights to the George Bernard Shaw plays), theatrical impresario Jed Harris, and the distinguished documentary filmmaker Pare Lorentz.

None of the deals were as liberal as Welles's, but, of course, Welles, the boy wonder of the theater and architect of the "War of the Worlds" broadcast, was by far the biggest prize. To get him, Schaefer violated one of the most sacred canons of the industry. In granting Welles the right of final cut, he allowed creative considerations to take priority over the studio's means of protecting its financial investment. The entire arrangement was bitterly resented in the industry at the time, and ever after the Hollywood trade press missed no opportunity to roast Schaefer or to take a shot at Welles. For instance, when Schaefer announced a pay cut for studio employees, James R. Wilkerson, editor of *Hollywood Reporter,* wrote in his influential column "Trade Views":

> If Mr. George Schaefer had come out with an announcement, occasioned by the withdrawal of financing by the Odlum interests, that the Orson Welles picture was too much of a gamble to take during these critical times and he had prevailed on Mr. Welles to step back his production effort for a while, the RKO president would have been a big guy in town yesterday. But Mr. Schaefer evidently does not think an investment of $750,000 or more with an untried producer, writer, director, with a questionable story and a rumored cast of players who, for the most part, have never seen a camera, is a necessary cut in these critical times.[3]

Welles's subsequent performance at RKO provided adequate opportunity for those in the industry and press to say "I told you so." But through it all Schaefer never lost his faith in his original commitment. Welles had direct access to Schaefer. Studio records show him appealing time and time again to Schaefer for support in a dispute with the studio hierarchy, for further indulgence, or for another chance. In a number of these cases, some involving very crucial matters, cold business judgment alone would seem to dictate that Welles be dealt with more firmly or even cut off. Sometimes Schaefer implies to other studio personnel that that is what he is going to do. Yet almost invariably he ends up supporting Welles or giving him roughly what he wants. The simple fact seems to be that Schaefer believed Welles was going to pull off something really big almost as much as Welles did himself. It was an unusual kind of daring and all the more surprising since Schaefer's background was almost exclusively in film distribution, not production. (Welles seems to have thought of Schaefer as one more Hollywood lowbrow who could be swayed by an artistic reputation.) In the end, it was Schaefer's faith in Welles more than any other factor that led to his own downfall at RKO. The other two major ventures on which he and Welles were involved after *Citizen Kane, The Magnificent Ambersons* and *It's All True,* were both total disasters from the industry standpoint, and both Schaefer and

Welles soon found themselves out in the street. But one of their projects paid off triumphantly, and it should be stated unequivocally for the historical record that without Schaefer's gamble and continued trust in his own instincts on Welles, *Citizen Kane* would never have been possible.

By prearrangement in his contract, Welles's first film was to be an adaptation of *Heart of Darkness,* Joseph Conrad's novel about a Byronic superhero and symbol of Western imperialism who sets up a diabolical empire deep in the African jungle. The Mercury Theatre had done *Heart of Darkness* as a radio show, and it was the kind of prestige literary property that carried special weight with Schaefer. The subject matter also had a special appeal for Welles. Again and again in his films, he would return to the dramatic situation of a morally transcendent hero, excessive and compulsively self-destructive, who is an object of veneration and awe to a lesser man — Kane and Leland, Arkadin and Van Stratten, Quinlan and Menzies, even Falstaff and Prince Hal. As Naremore has shown, the pattern was set as early as *Bright Lucifer,* a play that Welles wrote in his teens. Welles himself undertook the screenplay.[4] The first draft was quite literally taken from the source novel: The *Heart of Darkness* pages were removed from copies of the popular paperback collection *Great Modern Short Stories* and pasted individually onto sheets of typing paper, and Welles worked his way through these, marking the passages that were to be retained and crossing out the rest. Occasionally he changed or added a line or two, and he drew a few rough visual sketches in the margins, but at this stage it was essentially the kind of adapting they did for the radio shows — lifting voice-over material and a few playable scenes virtually intact from the original.

Conrad's Marlow narratives do not adapt easily to the screen. Though a great many richly adventurous things happen to Marlow, the yield in cinematic terms is low. This is because of the way Marlow tells his stories — he is very sparing with concrete details, he prefers to summarize rather than to dramatize, and he likes to envelop what he reports in lengthy metaphysical disquisitions and musings. The outward look of events is suppressed, since what happens is of less interest than what it is made out to be — or as the unnamed narrator in *Heart of Darkness* puts it, ·

The yarns of seamen have a direct simplicity, the whole meaning of which lies within the shell of a cracked nut. But Marlow was not typical (if his propensity to spin yarns be excepted), and to him the meaning of an episode was not inside like a kernel but outside, enveloping the tale which brought it out only as a glow brings out a haze.[5]

Welles's foremost problem in adapting *Heart of Darkness* was to reverse Conrad's method and externalize the story while at the same time remaining faithful to Conrad's spirit. In a sense, he had to fill in Marlow's vast silences and make them dramatically palpable.

The form Welles adopted was a compromise. He kept the frame story with Marlow as voice-over narrator and retained a generous portion of his broodings on the sea and the eternal verities virtually intact; these appear in the screenplay much as Welles blocked them out in the pasteups. He also followed the basic

In Welles's original conception, the river was to be the most important visual and thematic element in the *Heart of Darkness* film. As Marlow and company moved inland from the mouth toward the source, the river and the surrounding jungle would go through six distinct stages. In the first stage (sketch above), the jungle is "at its biggest and healthiest. Enormous, impenetrable, lofty, teeming with life, loud with the sound of birds. Apparently uninhabited by natives. The river is still broad enough so that we can see where the line of the bank meets the water at the side of the boat, so that it is necessary to pull into shore to get to Station Number Two."

storyline of the original but freely permuted characterizations, motivations, and plot incidents. The story is updated to the present. Marlow is made an American; the opening is set in New York harbor. The river and continent of the main action are unnamed, and the company employing Marlow is owned by an unnamed foreign government. Kurtz is being sent for to return and assume some kind of political leadership role. Parallels are repeatedly drawn between Kurtz's leadership style and contemporary fascist regimes in Europe. A whole cast of characters joins Marlow on the trip up river. Some have a rough basis in the faceless bureaucrats of Conrad's novel, but the characterizations themselves are mostly invented. There are nine in all, assorted company men and a halfbreed steersman. They are reminiscent of the collections of gargoyles and grotesques one finds later in *The*

In the second stage, the river narrows, bringing the jungle oppressively close to the boat. The air is humid and sickly sweet, and the animal life is restricted to crocodiles and snakes. In the third, the river narrows again, thick undergrowth covers the banks, and the water turns into a kind of liquid mud that is shallow and full of snags. The surrounding vegetation, all bamboo, cane, brush, and scrub, has been dried out by the relentless sun, and everything seems dead. In the fourth stage (sketch above), "dryness gives way to dead rot. Bamboos to willows, then willows to cypress. The river seems to be nothing but a place cut out of this ghostly world by the steamer itself. The water is no longer rich with mud and until the steamer breaks it up it is clear and still and black-looking. This is a place where the jungle has crawled to in order to die."

Lady from Shanghai, Mr. Arkadin, and *Touch of Evil.* The most interesting is de Tirpitz, a faded aristocrat of the type Erich von Stroheim often played, who secretly hates Kurtz and all his lower-middle-class kind and thinks he should be shot instead of rescued. Elsa, Kurtz's fiancée, also goes along as far as the Third Station, but Marlow decides that things are too dangerous and sends her back. Not surprisingly, Marlow falls in love with her. The dying Kurtz suggests that Marlow take his place with her. There are extravagant spectacle and expressionist touches typical of a Welles production. Three thousand black natives are to be seen bowing down to Kurtz in the jungle. (An alarmed production executive pointed out to Schaefer that there were only four or five hundred black extras registered in all Hollywood.)[6] At the heart of darkness is a lake, and at its center is a temple set on poles, its interior decorated with human skulls and bones. Kurtz turns de Tirpitz

Toward the end of the fourth stage are groves of dead cypress trees "festooned with moss and tangled with the withered strings of vines" (sketch above). In the fifth, the river becomes a marsh, and dead trees lie uprooted in the water. The sky is "swollen and dark," and the atmosphere is one of "unearthly gloom." In the sixth stage, the river all but disappears as it nears its source, and the boat almost seems to be gliding over a surface of dry scrub and brush. (In the shooting script, this is the section of the jungle that burns.)

The quotations are from the Story Outline of September 1, 1939; sketches by Charles Ohmann. In late September, Welles sent assistant director Eddie Donahoe and art director Walter Keller to scout possible locations for the river terrain in the Florida Everglades and Panama, but eventually he had to abandon the six-stage idea as unworkable.

over to the natives, and next day they appear displaying his head on the end of a pole. As the boat starts back, the jungle goes up in flames around them. Kurtz's image is present in the background throughout Marlow's final meeting with Elsa, and as Marlow tells her the lie about Kurtz's death, Kurtz is heard repeating over and over again, "The horror! The horror!" Typically, Welles and his people maintained that even his most drastic changes were true to the original and what Conrad himself "would desire done in a film if he were alive today."[7]

Welles wrote the character parts with specific actors, mostly Mercury Theatre people, in mind. Gus Schilling, Jack Carter, Edgar Barrier, Erskine Sanford, Norman Lloyd, Frank Readick, George Coulouris, Ray Collins, Everett Sloane, and John Emery (a Shakespearean actor who was to play de Tirpitz; he was married to Tallulah Bankhead) were all signed and put on salary for an October 10 starting

Kurtz enthroned in his temple in the middle of the lake at the heart of darkness. This setting and the idea of placing the first encounter with Kurtz in it were Welles's invention. The interior walls are like the cyclorama of skulls used in the Mercury Theatre production of *Danton's Death;* see Richard France, *Theatre of Orson Welles,* for a photograph.

Welles and assistant director Eddie Donahoe discussing the action on a model of
the temple set.

date. This was later postponed to October 31, and then, with most of them already
in Hollywood and ready to begin work, it was postponed again. One reason for the
delay was that Welles was giving considerably less than full energy to the project.
He was still doing the radio shows in New York Sunday nights, which meant that
he divided his time each week between the two coasts; a full day was required for
travel each way.[8] Another reason was the complicated approach to shooting Welles
had decided on. Welles wanted to remain as faithful as possible to Conrad's first-
person form of narration. In conventional filmmaking, this would have meant the
use of certain visual cues and camera placements through which subjective view-
point could be implied. In contrast, Welles devised a narrational strategy that
would literally simulate Marlow's point of view. The camera would actually be a
character in the story — it would have its own voice, it would imitate human physical movement, and the other characters would play to it as if it were another
person. (Welles had accomplished a parallel innovation in radio technique with his
use of first-person narrators who were also involved in the story.) To underline the
effect, Marlow's shadow would sometimes be seen on the wall. The camera would
register the flow of events continuously, without cuts, as human consciousness
would. This meant that the camera would have to move through doorways, up and
down stairways, into and out of close quarters — wherever the character would go.

Charles Ohmann's panoramic sketch of the First Station in *Heart of Darkness.*
Ohmann's sketch is based on passages slightly abridged from Conrad: "At last we
opened a reach. A cliff appeared, mounds of turned-up earth by the shore, houses on
a hill, with iron roofs, amongst a waste of excavations. A jetty projected into the
river. A blinding sunlight drowned all this at times in a sudden recrudescence of
glare." "A boiler wallowing in the grass, a path leading up the hill. It turned aside for
an undersized railway-truck lying there on its back with its wheels in the air. One
was off. The thing looked as dead as the carcass of some animal. I came upon more
pieces of decaying machinery, a stack of rusty rails." Welles added: "A nasty, wide
beach of mud. Sheds of corrugated tin, standing on short legs stuck into the mud."
He also placed the broken-down steamboat that will take Marlow upriver here rather
than at the Second Station, thus eliminating the long overland trek described in the
novel (Story Outline, September 1, 1939).

Sketch artist Albert Pyke's reverse angle view of the scene from the docks at the
First Station.

The most difficult and ambitious sequence would involve Marlow's arrival at the First Station. This is the key event of the first part of the novel: Marlow gets his first real foretaste of the horrors to come when he walks up the hill past the excavations and stumbles across the place where the native laborers have crawled to die. As Welles envisioned it, Marlow as the camera was to proceed up the hill from the docks, pass the excavations, discover the dying natives, enter the settlement, see Elsa, go to the British representative's quarters, have a conversation, retrace his steps through the settlement to the manager's office, and have another conversation there — all continuously and without an apparent cut. To solve the problem of getting Marlow from one place to another without having laboriously to document his movements, Welles came up with an experimental device they called the feather wipe. This involved panning the camera to a stationary point, repositioning the camera but directing it to the same point, then continuing the pan in a new shot. For instance, if Marlow was standing on the deck of a boat that had just docked, his eyes would pan to the side of a building on shore. The pan would continue in the new shot and come to rest as Marlow engaged in conversation

An elevated model of the First Station scene. Eddie Donahoe, assistant director, holds the little periscope they used to visualize how things would appear to the camera. Looking on with Welles are (pipe in hand) Freddie Fleck, another assistant director, and (holding pencil) Mercury publicist Herbert Drake.

on the docks. The two shots would be precision framed — that is, the distance between the camera and the transitional texture or object was measured so that it would be exactly the same in both shots to disguise the fact that a cut had occurred.

Welles at work on *Heart of Darkness*. In the background is a sketch for the film's prologue, in which Welles was to introduce the audience to the first-person camera device. To Welles's explanatory narration, the camera would adopt the points of view, successively, of a bird in a cage, a condemned man about to be electrocuted, and a golfer driving a ball. Then it would take Welles's point of view from the screen, looking into a movie audience made up entirely of motion picture cameras. In the final shot, an eye would appear on the left side of a black screen, then the equals sign, then the pronoun I. The eye would wink, and a dissolve would lead to the opening shot of the film.

Welles knew what he wanted, but he had trouble expressing it in language and form that the technical and crafts people could recognize and understand. A script written in the accepted idiom would be necessary so that exact camera, set, special effects, and other requirements could be determined and a budget estimate derived. At this point, a junior-level technical assignment was made that would have very fortuitous consequences for Welles. Amalia Kent, a veteran Hollywood script supervisor since the 1920s, was brought onto the project from within RKO ranks. Kent had a reputation for being one of the best in the industry at her specialty, which was to convert the script material as it came from writers (in which form it was often very literary in nature) into a visual continuity suitable for budgeting and other forms of production planning and eventually for shooting. Essentially, her job involved the working out of an efficient set of mechanics for the actions described. Kent worked directly with Welles at the private residence that temporarily housed the Mercury operation. Welles gave her his copy of the script (she recalls that it was a complete draft) and described the intended camera operations at great length. Using this, and occasionally resorting to a little periscope they used to work out the more complicated movements on elevated models of the sets, she turned out a complete first draft with all the mechanics indicated in the accepted form in short order. (Welles found Kent's work so valuable that he insisted on her for all his subsequent projects while at RKO. She would see a script completely through its written development, then serve as continuity supervisor during the shooting.) This 202-page script was mimeographed on November 7 and delivered to budgeting. A copy was also sent to Schaefer in New York, who responded guardedly that he was "sure it will make a very unusual picture"; however, he wondered whether there might not be an excess of dialogue (he is probably referring to the Conradian voice-overs as well as to the conversations) or whether drawing the contemporary political parallels was wise.[9] Meanwhile, Welles proceeded with plans for some test shooting. There were four days of tests. Linwood Dunn, who had been brought in to deal with the special effects problems that the script posed, recalls that the action involved a "bar in the tropics"; by this he means the scene at the First Station in which Marlow first meets Elsa.[10] Kent, who was also present, says it was an enormously laborious and time-consuming process because of the elaborate camera movements and the intricate repositionings and measurements needed for the feather wipes.[11]

The preliminary budget, completed December 5, showed a total estimated picture cost of $1,057,761. The news would have come as a double shock to Schaefer. Not only was it more than twice the target amount specified in Welles's contract, but it came on the heels of a financial crisis at RKO that had developed in the meantime. Faced with the prospect of lost revenues as a result of the war situation in Europe, Schaefer had lowered the maximum limit on picture costs in late September and imposed an across-the-board salary reduction on RKO employees. At the time, he sent a personal wire to Welles painting the situation in the gloomiest terms and pleading with him to do everything possible to keep the budget down on *Heart of Darkness*. In a written analysis of the budget, Schaefer's Hollywood people advised him that substantial reductions were unlikely without cuts in the script. They also informed him that, because of the unusual shooting methods, the bulk of the special effects work would have to be done first and the principal photography matched with it, rather than the customary other way around; this would require twelve to fourteen weeks, which meant that Welles would not be able to commence principal photography until mid March at the earliest.[12] (All this had been explained to Welles, who bowed to the inevitable and informed his actors that they would be taken off salary on December 10.) Welles was on his way to New York when Schaefer got the news. They met there on Saturday, December 9, and out of their discussion came the outlines of a substantially new agreement that was intended to rescue the project.

Welles would make another picture before *Heart of Darkness*. It would be a more commercially viable property, and it would cost no more than $400,000. It would star Carole Lombard (who had an informal agreement with RKO to do an occasional picture when a suitable vehicle turned up) if she agreed. It would go into production as soon as possible and be completed by April 1, 1940. It would then be pledged as collateral against further financing of *Heart of Darkness*. Meanwhile, RKO would proceed with the necessary special effects work, and Welles would try to cut at least $250,000 out of the *Heart of Darkness* budget. *Heart of Darkness* would then go into production by May 1. Welles (at his own insistence) would receive no additional compensation for services on the new picture, but (at Schaefer's insistence) he would receive the 20 percent share of the profits called for in his original contract. He would also make a third unspecified picture (the second picture called for in the original contract), to begin production during calendar year 1940.[13] In effect, Welles bought time for *Heart of Darkness* with a two-for-one trade.

The property on which Welles sold Schaefer was *The Smiler With the Knife,* an espionage thriller by C. Day Lewis just published under his pseudonym Nicholas Blake. Its subject matter was the currently popular topic of enemy agents infiltrating innocent domestic regimes. A fascist organization is using an oddball but harmless secret aristocratic society as a front for a conspiracy to take over the British Isles and install a fascist dictatorship. A prominent citizen, Georgia Strangeways, is recruited by Scotland Yard (reluctantly on her part, since it means temporarily separating from her husband and giving up her comfortable seclusion in the country) to penetrate the organization and uncover the plot. Sir Chilton Canteloe, a distinguished aristocrat, suave and handsome, and a leading benefactor of worthy causes, is the secret leader of the cabal. Predictably, the heroine must place herself in great danger, but she escapes at the last minute, and the conspiracy is exposed. An RKO reader summarized, "there is not much that is original" in the story, "but it has a pleasant heroine and a timeliness of plot which might make it the material for a very exciting picture of the Hitchcock variety."[14]

The novel had been purchased for Welles's use and Welles and Kent were well along on the screenplay at the time of his meeting with Schaefer. He changed the setting to America and reshaped the story more along the lines of a screwball comedy. In his version, the heroine, Gloria Corbett, is a madcap heiress. As she and her fiancé wait for a country parson to marry them, a crow lands on a window sill and drops a locket from its beak. Later, in Washington, the groom's father, who is head of the U.S. Secret Service, recognizes it as an emblem used by Nazi conspirators and enlists his new daughter-in-law's help to uncover the conspiracy. The chief suspect is Anthony Chilton, a handsome and wealthy playboy industrialist who takes a special interest in experimental aviation. (Welles told me he modeled this character on Howard Hughes. This is the source for the puzzling claim in Welles's film *F for Fake* that Hughes was his target before Hearst.) The newlyweds stage a fight and separate so that she will be free to pursue the suspect unimpeded. A cross-country chase ensues once she is found out (including a sequence set in the Midwest at Todd's School for Boys, Welles's boyhood school), but justice triumphs, and the couple celebrate by being married a second time. The ending sports a Lubitsch touch: As the ceremony is about to begin, a second crow alights on the window sill with something in its beak, but the groom shoos it away before the object drops.

At Schaefer's direction, the *Smiler* script was sent to Carole Lombard, who turned it down. Welles then asked for Lucille Ball, but Schaefer was unwilling to gamble on her in a leading role. Shortly after the first of the year, a postponement was announced, and the project was allowed to die.[15] The official reason given at the time (and often repeated by Welles, among others) was the failure to locate a suitable actress. However, it is hard to see how this type of material could have held Welles's creative attention for very long. Besides, after all the fanfare a B comedy thriller would have been a very modest beginning indeed.

Rather than continue the effort to save *Heart of Darkness,* Welles let it die quietly, too. Several explanations have been advanced. One is the reason given for not going ahead with *Smiler With the Knife* — the actress he wanted for Elsa, Dita Parlo, could not get out of Europe because of the war situation. This explanation can be traced to an item in *Variety* announcing the first postponement of the project.[16] Actually, the problem referred to there was later cleared up, and Parlo would have been contracted if *Heart of Darkness* had proceeded.[17] Another reason that was given was the primitive state of hand-held cameras. This explanation probably originated with the Mercury publicity unit as a face-saving device. While camera technology may have posed a very real problem, it was only one of many. Welles himself told me there was one explanation clear and simple — the cost. Yet at the time of the two-for-one agreement, Welles assured Schaefer that he could reduce the budget substantially and indicated he was already getting valuable help from screenwriting veteran Gene Towne on ways of going about it. If Welles was sincere, surely Schaefer, in view of his disposition in Welles's favor, could have been convinced one more time. A more likely explanation is that Welles gave up on *Heart of Darkness* because he had gone as far as he could with it on his own. He had approached *Heart of Darkness* like a Mercury radio or stage production, making the important creative decisions by himself and leaving it up to the talent pool to implement them. But the technical and story problems involved in

Heart of Darkness as he wanted to make it were beyond the capabilities of Welles and the staff. This does not mean that they were necessarily beyond solution: It is intriguing to imagine what the outcome would have been if, say, Gregg Toland had been turned loose with the problem of the first-person camera. Welles had, however, failed to enlist people of Toland's caliber for the project. As a consequence, he was without the kind of top-notch professional and technical people who might have been counted on to come up with workable solutions.

It was now five months — as much time as some Hollywood veterans needed to do a whole picture — and there was not even a story idea in hand. As each day passed, the unthinkable became a more distinct possibility: Not only might Welles not deliver the something big that everyone was expecting; he might not deliver at all. *Hollywood Reporter* could not pass up an opportunity to twist the knife: "They are laying bets over on the RKO lot that the Orson Welles deal will end up without Orson ever doing a picture there. The whole thing seems to be so mixed up no one can unravel it. You can get better odds that the original Welles announcement, *Heart of Darkness,* won't ever be done, and can get 50–1 that neither Dita Parlo nor Lucille Ball will ever go into the second announced picture, *Smiler With a Knife.* The impression is that the current Welles confab with Schaefer in New York may end up the whole works."[18] It was in this atmosphere of extreme urgency that the idea for *Citizen Kane* came into being.

2

Scripting

Welles's first step toward the realization of *Citizen Kane* was to seek the assistance of a screenwriting professional. Fortunately, help was near at hand. Writing talent had always been in short supply in the Mercury operation because of the inexorable demands of the weekly radio shows. When Welles moved to Hollywood, it happened that a veteran screenwriter, Herman J. Mankiewicz, was recuperating from an automobile accident and between jobs. Mankiewicz was signed to write scripts for the Mercury's "Campbell Playhouse" radio program. When the opportunity to work on a screenplay for the Mercury presented itself, Mankiewicz was still available, and he took on this additional assignment as well.[1]

Mankiewicz was an expatriate from Broadway who had been writing for films for almost fifteen years. He had anticipated a trend in 1926 when, as an aspiring young writer, critic, and playwright, he had answered Hollywood's call. Unlike others who took seasonal contracts and used their lucrative screenwriting salaries to support what they regarded as their real work back East, Mankiewicz stayed on and worked almost exclusively in films until his death in 1953. In the early years, he mainly wrote intertitles for silent films. After sound came in, he did his best work in comedy. His credits include select specimens of sophisticated dialogue comedy (*Laughter, Royal Family of Broadway, Dinner at Eight*) and of the anarchic farce associated especially with the Marx Brothers (*Monkey Business, Horse Feathers*) and W. C. Fields (*Million Dollar Legs*). In his film work, Mankiewicz was never known as a distance runner; in all the examples just cited, he received either screenplay co-credit or some special form of billing, such as associate producer. In contrast, writers like Ben Hecht and Samson Raphaelson were getting sole or top screenwriting billing on their best comedy scripts. Mankiewicz hit his peak in 1934 and 1935, when he received sole screenwriter credit on four films at MGM — *The Show-off* (with Spencer Tracy), *Stamboul Quest* (with Myrna Loy and George Brent), *After Office Hours* (with Clark Gable), and *Escapade* (with Luise Rainer, who was making her American debut). After that, his output fell dramatically. Between 1935 and the time when he was assigned to *Citizen Kane,* he received screenplay credit on only two films.[2] Not that this state of affairs was really disadvantageous to Welles. He lacked the patience that original story construction requires. He preferred to start with a rough diamond and do just the cutting and polishing himself. Besides, a more secure and better-established writer would almost certainly insist on prerogatives. As things stood, Mankiewicz was hardly in a position to make demands.

Whether Welles or Mankiewicz came up with the idea for a send-up of William Randolph Hearst is a matter of dispute. Welles claims he did. The Mankiewicz partisans — chiefly Pauline Kael (and through her Mankiewicz's widow Sara) and John Houseman — say it was the other way around. Kael maintains that Mankiewicz had been toying with the idea for years. She reports the testimony of a former Mankiewicz baby-sitter that she took dictation from Mankiewicz on a flashback screenplay involving Hearst even before he went to Hollywood.[3] Houseman, who had broken with Welles and the Mercury by this time, writes in his memoirs that Welles sought him out in New York and pleaded with him to come back and help with a screenplay idea that, Welles said, had been proposed by Mankiewicz. The conversation is said to have taken place at "21" shortly after the first of the year in 1940.[4] But in an affidavit taken at the time of the film's release, Mercury assistant Richard Baer swore that the original idea was first broached by Welles at the "21" luncheon and that Welles and Houseman, who agreed to sign on, approached Mankiewicz about it back in California.[5] We will probably never know for sure, but in any case Welles had at last found a subject with the right combination of monumentality, timeliness, and audacity. Lampooning Hearst was nothing new; he had been at the center of controversy for his entire public life. But in the 1930s it became commonplace to question or even attack the older ideal of America and the system of values that Hearst represented. (Even FDR spoke out against the possessors of "self-serving wealth," such as Hearst, branding them enemies of the republic and obstacles to social reform.) Nor was the tabloid angle on Hearst's personal life as original a stroke as it has been made out to be. In his 1939 novel *After Many a Summer Dies the Swan,* Aldous Huxley had been far nastier in his insinuations about Hearst and Marion Davies than anything in the *Citizen Kane* scripts. What was new was to take on Hearst from within Hollywood, where he had enormous influence and power to retaliate and was almost universally feared.

For obvious reasons, the project needed to be kept as quiet as possible. Consequently, it was decided that Mankiewicz would do his work away from Hollywood. There was another motive for this, too: Mankiewicz had a drinking problem (the main cause of his career decline). Houseman would go along to provide assistance but also to keep Mankiewicz out of trouble and on course. Mankiewicz went on the RKO payroll on February 19, 1940. He was to receive $1,000 a week, with a bonus of $5,000 on delivery of the script. During the last week in February or the first week in March, he and Houseman, together with a secretary, Rita Alexander, went into seclusion at a guest ranch in the desert at Victorville, California, several hours' drive from Hollywood. There, during March, April, and early May 1940, the first installments of the *Citizen Kane* script were written. First and second drafts were completed during this period. Alexander took them down from Mankiewicz's dictation; Houseman served as editor. In his lengthy account of the Victorville interlude, Houseman gives the impression that Mankiewicz started out with a clean slate and that virtually everything in the Victorville drafts is Mankiewicz's original invention.[6] Kael made the same assumption. In arguing the case for Mankiewicz's authorship, she placed a great deal of emphasis on prior activities that were circumstantially parallel — for instance, that he had written unproduced screenplays based on Aimee Semple McPherson and John Dillinger that employed the device of multiple narration.[7] For his part, Welles says he had lengthy discussions with Mankiewicz about the story before Mankiewicz left for Victorville. (He concludes that Mankiewicz never admitted this to Houseman or anyone else involved.) Welles gave Bogdanovich some examples of story incidents in the script he said originated with him.[8] By looking into Welles's past for evidence, as Kael did into Mankiewicz's, we come up with other possibilities that would seem to substantiate his claim. For instance, the unmade *Smiler With the Knife* would also have been an attack on a controversial contemporary figure. In fact, in Welles's script, the Howard Hughes figure would have been introduced to an audience in the film by means of a "March of Time" newsreel feature. There is another set of tantalizing parallels: A 1936 "March of Time" radio broadcast included an obituary of munitions tycoon Sir Basil Zaharoff, with invented dramatic episodes. In the opening scene, secretaries are burning Zaharoff's papers in the immense fireplace in the great hall of his chateau — the secret records (the narrator tells us) of a lifetime's involvement in wars, plots, revolutions, and assassinations. Other scenes present witnesses who testify to Zaharoff's ruthlessness. Finally, Zaharoff himself appears — an old man nearing death, alone except for servants in the gigantic palace in Monte Carlo that he had acquired for his longtime mistress. His dying wish is to be wheeled out "in the sun by that rosebush." Welles played Zaharoff.[9]

THE VICTORVILLE SCRIPTS

In mid April, after six weeks of work, Mankiewicz and Houseman sent down a first rough draft. More than 250 pages long, *American,* as it was called, was what rough drafts usually are — excessive in content and lacking in focus. But nevertheless it provided what was most needed at this stage: a firm story structure on which to build.

American is the biography of a publishing tycoon and public figure told in retrospect after his death by the persons who had known him best. A similar plot premise had been used in *The Power and the Glory* (1933), directed by William K. Howard from a script by Preston Sturges, in which Spencer Tracy portrayed a controversial railroad magnate who was revered by a faithful few but detested by the many. One of the main weaknesses of that film is the cumbrousness of its flashback structure. To compensate for this tendency of multiple flashback plots, Mankiewicz came up with an ingeniously simple plot device — a mysterious deathbed utterance that is presumed to be the key to everything. Rosebud is a rather shameless piece of melodramatic gimmickry, but it is arguably a more effective narrative device than Welles's original idea of making the object of mystery something literary, such as a line from a Romantic poem. (Welles has always ceded the Rosebud gimmick to Mankiewicz.)

Use of the glass snow scene ball at Kane's death may have been inspired by another RKO film, *Kitty Foyle* (1940). At his death, Kitty's father drops a little glass globe with a snow scene inside and it rolls to the floor at his feet. The glass globes for both films were built in the RKO property department.

Equally as important as Rosebud is the cast of supporting characters, a gallery of stereotypes, admittedly, but an interesting and very serviceable variety: parents of humble origin from the West, a Wall Street tycoon, a pragmatic business manager, a stuffy first wife of enormous social standing, a somewhat dandified closest friend, and a shopgirl mistress.

About two-thirds of the way through *American*, there is a large story gap — probably an indication that the draft sent down at someone's insistence was incomplete. The missing portion would come to include all of Kane's early relationship with Susan — their meeting, the love nest, their marriage, her singing career. But after the gap, *American* resumes with another firm plot situation, the elderly Kane withdrawn with Susan to Xanadu, and it concludes with the identification of the rosebud clue for the audience.

Structurally, *American* has roughly the narrative order that the final *Kane* shooting script will have, and some of the material (especially in the first third) will remain substantially the same. But there are also some serious problems. To begin with, considerable paring is needed. Many scenes are undeveloped, superfluous, or merely dull. Among the most expendable material in *American* are scenes of Thatcher visiting Kane at his Renaissance palace in Rome on his twenty-fifth birthday to discuss the future management of Kane's interest; of Kane's honeymoon with Emily in the remote Wisconsin woods, with an army of chefs and

AMERICAN

FADE IN

A VAST GATEWAY OF GRILLED IRON

(In the middle of which is clearly seen a huge initial
"K") stretching clear across the road. As the CAMERA
MOVES toward it, the gate opens and the CAMERA PASSES
through. A few feet further on, the gate having closed
behind it, the CAMERA REVEALS, either because it has
reached the top of a small incline or because it has
turned a bend, (depending upon the topography to be
selected).

THE LITERALLY INCREDIBLE DOMAIN

Of Charles Foster Kane. Its right flank resting for
nearly forty miles on the Gulf Coast, it truly extends
in all directions farther than the eye can see. Designed
by nature to be almost completely bare and flat -- it was,
as will develop, practically all marsh-land when Kane
acquired it and changed its face -- it is now pleasantly
uneven, with its fair share of rolling hills and one very
good-sized mountain, all man-made. Almost all the land is
improved, either through cultivation for farming purposes
or through careful landscaping, in the shape of parks and
lakes. The castle itself, an enormous pile, compounded
of several genuine castles, of European origin, of varying
architecture -- dominates the scene, from the very peak of
the mountain.

                                        DISSOLVE

GOLF LINKS

Past which we move. The greens are straggly and overgrown,
the fairways wild with tropical weeds, the links unused
and not seriously tended for a long time.

                                        DISSOLVE

SIX CHAMPIONSHIP-SIZED TENNIS COURTS

Only one is in even fair condition. The others have torn
and sagging nets, there are fissures in the cement,
baselines have been obliterated. The one court alone
clearly has been used, and that not too carefully, to the
exclusion of the others, for a long time.

                                        DISSOLVE OUT

The first page of *American*, the first draft of the *Citizen Kane* screenplay. The
idea of opening with the camera slowly moving in on a dilapidated estate (also the
use of a monogram) may have come from *Rebecca*, which began previewing in Hollywood in December 1939.

servants in attendance (Kane's yacht, which had to be shipped up piece by piece and reassembled, is anchored in a small lake nearby); of a subplot involving Kane and the president, an oil scandal, and an inflammatory editorial that leads to an assassination attempt; of a chance meeting between Kane and his father at the theater one evening, the latter in the company of a "young tart" who turns out to be his new wife; of Kane's discovery of an affair between Susan and a young lover at Xanadu (Kane has him killed);[10] and of the funeral of Kane's son (he was shot when he and other members of a fascist movement staged a raid on an armory in Washington). (See the Appendix for art department sketches of some of these scenes.) For another thing, much of the material in *American* lacks convincing dramatic motivation. Several key events are still early in gestation. Since most of the Susan material has not been written, there is no love nest to expose, and Kane's crooked opponents conspire to steal the election from him. Leland goes to Chicago not because of the election but because of an affront to his integrity as drama critic: a new policy, apparently instituted with Kane's blessing, to guarantee favorable notices to producers for their shows in exchange for advertising considerations. When Susan sings in Chicago, Leland passes out at his typewriter before finishing the review, but instead of having Kane finish it for him (an inspired touch), a box is run on the theatrical page saying the review will be a day late (the way it really happened to Mankiewicz once when he was a second-stringer on the *New York Times*). There are also internal inconsistencies. For instance, Emily is still alive in 1940, but she refuses to be interviewed; yet her part of the story appears at the appropriate place anyway, without a narrator. By far the most serious dramatic problem in *American* is its portrait of Kane. Mankiewicz drew a good deal of his material directly from Hearst without really assimilating it to dramatic need. There is a large amount of Hearst material in *Citizen Kane* — for instance, his scandalmongering, his ideological inconsistencies, San Simeon, the vast collections of everything under the sun, the awkwardness of his May– December romance with Marion Davies, even some of his memorable lines — but this is nothing approaching what is in the Mankiewicz script. *American* is by and large a literal reworking of specific incidents and details from Hearst's life. Much of it Mankiewicz knew on his own. As a former newspaper reporter, he had the professional's familiarity with all the great legends of journalism's most colorful era. As a privileged visitor to San Simeon, Mankiewicz would have observed firsthand such things as Marion Davies's tippling, her passion for jigsaw puzzles, Hearst's fondness for arranging elaborate picnic outings, and so on.

But it is clear that Mankiewicz also borrowed from published accounts of Hearst. He always denied it, claiming all his information was firsthand, but coincidences between *American* and Ferdinand Lundberg's *Imperial Hearst* are hard to explain. Lundberg reports that Hearst's father acquired the *San Francisco Examiner* in 1880 for a bad debt of $100,000 — precisely the amount Thatcher is offered for the *Enquirer* (thus spelled in *American*) after he acquires it in a foreclosure proceeding. Lundberg describes Hearst's phenomenal success in his first years in newspaper publishing and offers as a landmark the fact that by 1889 the *Examiner*

In 1935, Hearst retaliated against a proposed boycott of his newspapers by purchasing advertising space in rival papers and publishing a statement of principles. This was probably the basis for the incident in *Citizen Kane* when Kane draws up and boldly signs his "Declaration of Principles."

had reached a Sunday circulation of 62,000. In *American,* when the *Enquirer*'s circulation reaches the 62,000 figure, Kane has it painted on a huge sign outside his rival's window. Lundberg reports that Hearst actually won his 1905 campaign for mayor of New York City:

Hearst won the election. He was the victor by several thousand votes, it has since been established, but the Tammany bruisers, heeding their instructions from Murphy, went berserk. Hearst's campaign people were assaulted and ballot boxes were stolen from the Hearst wards and dumped into the East River.[11]

Identical details appear in dramatized form in *American:*

Narrator:

On election day   A LITTLE MAN, in an overcoat, with a card in his hat reading, "Watcher," is being given the bum's rush out of a laundry. (Sign in the window of the laundry reads "Polling Booth.") A line of about twenty people is stretched outside the door, with a policeman guarding the head of the line. As the Watcher is dragged through the door, he stands his ground firmly and turns to the policeman. The policeman deliberately turns his back on him. The Watcher is dragged along.

SMALL BACK ROOM. Three men in overcoats and hats are sitting around the table. One has in front of him a huge pile of unfolded ballots.

MOONLIGHT. A row-boat in the East River. A man reaches into the bottom of the boat, brings up a ballot box, and, helped by another man, throws the box into the river.

To have played the material in *American* as written would have involved some serious problems of copyright infringement. Strictly from a legal standpoint, *American* would be unusable without massive revision. The problem also has a dramatic side. Hearst was too free and easy a source of information for an unsteady writer like Mankiewicz. Most of *American* is quite simply *à clef* plotting with only the barest effort at characterization. Kane himself at this stage is more an unfocused composite than a character portrait, a stand-in mouthing dialogue manufactured for some imaginary Hearst. In this sense, Hearst is one of the principal obstacles to the script's further development. Before any real progress with the characterization could be made, the ties to his life had to be cut. That process began immediately after *American* and continued to the end of scripting. A lot of Hearst material survives in the film, but it is far less than was there at the beginning. (Lundberg eventually brought suit anyway.)[12] One reason why Welles could later maintain so confidently that Kane was not Hearst may be that he had eliminated so much of Mankiewicz's Hearst material from the script that he imagined he had somehow eliminated Hearst in the process.

On April 28, less than two weeks after *American,* forty-four pages of revisions emanated from Victorville. Three very important changes appear in these pages.

A decision has been made about the part of the story Emily might have told—most of it is to be assigned to Leland—and the framing segments with Bernstein and Leland have been rewritten to reflect this change. The stolen election has been abandoned; now Kane actually loses. The cause is presented in two important new scenes—one in which Emily insists Kane pay a certain call with her after the Madison Square Garden rally and its sequel, the encounter in Kane and Susan's love nest.

By DAN WALKER
Footnotes to an Autobiography
Chapter VI

Backstage at the Wivel Restaurant, Evelyn Nesbit told me that after her debut as a member of the "Florodora" sextette—she was only 16 at the time and in constant dread of the Gerry Society—she was much in demand as an artists' model and her likeness appeared in many celebrated pictures, most popular of them being Charles Dana Gibson's pen-and-ink sketch, "The Eternal Question." When I told her I owned a famous photographic study of her, she was curious to know how it came into my possession, and I explained that it had been given me by friends from Detroit with whom I had spent a Winter in Western Florida; that this visit was the direct outgrowth of a scrape in which I, as a small boy, was shot by a friend while impersonating a man who had figured largely in her own unhappy past—Stanford White.

Mankiewicz's original source of inspiration (according to Houseman) for making Susan Alexander a washed-up singer and for having her interviewed at the nightclub where she performs was a column and interview with Evelyn Nesbit in the *New York Daily News*. Welles confirms the link with Evelyn Nesbit but says he never saw this item.

On or about May 9, Mankiewicz and Houseman completed their work at Victorville and returned to Hollywood with a second draft. Mankiewicz immediately went off to MGM on another assignment. Though he attempted to keep up with the revisions in the following weeks, he ceased to be a guiding hand in the *Citizen Kane* scripting process at this point. For this reason, it is important to look at the second draft carefully.

The most striking changes in the second draft involve Kane himself. Large chunks of material obviously based on Hearst have been removed. The stolen election is one example. Another involves Kane's educational history — how he was thrown out of college on account of a prank. Only one scene showing Kane with his publishing rivals remains. *American* had several tiresomely repetitive scenes intended to illustrate the libertine aspect of Kane's nature — Kane and Leland accompanied by women of questionable character at an expensive restaurant, Rector's, at the theater, and so on. This material has been considerably reduced in the second draft. The business of Susan's lover has also disappeared. Interesting scenes for Kane have been added — for instance, when Kane finds Leland passed out at his typewriter, he finishes the review himself, and when Susan leaves him, he smashes up her room. Other new scenes are not so fortunate — one, for instance, involving the burial of Kane's son in the chapel at Xanadu. Kane is overcome with grief. As he stares at the row of crypts, he begins to prattle about his mother, who also is buried there. He recalls how she loved poetry and begins to read the verse inscription on the wall.

Some individual narratives have been restructured, but the effect is more to bring out problems in the original material than to provide solutions. When what would have been Emily's story is shifted to Leland, one result is that he is now responsible for a disproportionate share of major episodes in Kane's life — the human side of Kane's early years as a crusading publisher, the entire story of Kane's marriage and its deterioration and breakup, Leland's growing disillusionment with Kane's compromise of his values, and their final break over the opera review. But there is an even more serious problem. Leland's narration is now loaded with dramatic crises — not only the two that were originally his, the shady promotional scheme and the opera debut, but three of Emily's — the assassination attempt, Susan, and the lost election. The difficulty stems from the nature of *American,* which is essentially a string of discrete events lifted from a colorful biography. Once the necessary process of rearranging begins, the dramatic unmanageability of such material becomes apparent. One of the main problems that subsequent revisions will face is how to deal with a large surplus of crisis moments.

A related difficulty appears in the new version of Bernstein's story. Several episodes are newly assigned to him, including Thatcher's angry encounter with Kane in the *Enquirer* office, the first installment of the opera review incident with Leland passed out at his typewriter (Leland later tells the sequel of Kane's finishing the review), scenes of Bernstein as an uncomfortable social guest at Xanadu, and the divestiture sequence in which Thatcher and company take control of Kane's newspapers. Apparently, the writers are considering whether a narrator ought to have firsthand knowledge of what he relates. If the answer is yes, serious structural imbalances will be created elsewhere (there are now no scenes between Thatcher and the adult Kane), and the pacing of events will be seriously disrupted (as when a dramatic tour de force like the opera review is broken up and shared between two narrators). Even partial fidelity to such a principle would create difficult problems for other parts of the story (Kane's intimate life with Emily, for instance). Eventually, it is sacrificed to the general principle that we ought to see a developing chronological view of Kane's life.

Elimination of redundant material, the addition of several new scenes between Kane and Susan, the inspired touch of the opera review, and the improvement of many passages of dialogue are among the main accomplishments of the second draft. But numerous difficulties still remain, especially with the portrait of Kane, and on balance the second draft might most justly be characterized as a much-improved rough draft.

WELLES AND THE LATER DRAFTS

Amalia Kent reworked the May 9 script into accepted continuity form, as she had done with the scripts for *Heart of Darkness* and *The Smiler With the Knife.* Copies were sent to Schaefer in New York, whose assent was needed to proceed, and to department heads so that planning could begin. Kent then prepared a breakdown script. This document contains only the scene designations and their physical descriptions. It allows the architectural values of a script to be separated from its literary values and formally stated for the purposes of budgeting the production. Once such information went into wider circulation, special precaution was needed to keep the secret under wraps. An informal conspiracy of silence began to be resolutely observed by all those immediately involved. Although it was obvious they were dealing with Hearst, no one spoke of this or acknowledged it unless it was strictly necessary in the course of work. There is one good reason why the silence worked so well despite the number of people involved: There were horror stories of how things that happened on sets somehow got back to Hearst and how even an unintentional offense could cost someone a career.[13] Schaefer was unfazed by the potential complications (he probably saw another "War of the Worlds" in the making, and his lawyers did not object to the script) and gave his approval. Welles's contracts were redrawn. The new agreement formalized the postponement of both *Heart of Darkness* and *Smiler With the Knife* and allowed Welles to proceed with this unnamed project first. It was to be completed by October 1, 1940, after which he would still owe the two pictures called for in the two-for-one compromise worked out on *Heart of Darkness.*[14]

Schaefer brought Welles East for an RKO sales meeting to assure skeptical distributors and exhibitors that he had something under way. Revisions on the Mankiewicz script resumed with great intensity after Welles returned to Holly-wood on June 1. During the first two weeks of June alone, around 140 pages were revised — more than half of the total script. When the budget estimate based on the Mankiewicz script came out in mid June, the working script with changes in progress was consolidated and identified as a new draft, the third. Altogether, more than 170 pages in this script had been added or revised since Welles had taken over the script in mid May.

Welles and Amalia Kent conferring on the *Citizen Kane* script during rehearsals.

The new draft eliminates around 75 pages of the Victorville scenes. Some had been intended to enhance character — Kane and Leland at Rector's with their girls, for instance. Others had been intended to foreshadow — scenes of Kane and Susan in Chicago for her opera debut, for instance, give privileged glimpses into their private relationship. Others were merely redundant — Kane and family and a group of politicians gathered to announce his entry into politics, Bernstein's appearances at Xanadu, and (perhaps the most outrageous episode in *American*) the appearance of Kane Senior and his young wife. The most dramatic changes made by Welles involved the collapsing of lengthy expository sequences played as straight dramatic interchanges into snappy and arresting montages. The circulation buildup, which originally had been played in encounters between rivals and in expository discussions between Kane and his associates, is now given in a montage: the composing room, the Declaration of Principles on a front page, a wagon with a sign "Enquirer: Circulation 26,000," various shots of the paper being delivered, a new number (62,000) being painted on the wall of a building, and Kane, Bernstein, and Leland looking at a *Chronicle* window display that includes a photograph of the rival paper's staff and a sign with its circulation figures. The scenes showing how Kane checkmated Thatcher and his cronies with pilfered documents have been eliminated, to be replaced by a three-and-a-half-page montage (expanded from a suggestion in *American*) of the *Enquirer*'s growing impact on the American scene in the 1890s. This montage ends with a close-up of Kane's passport (it reads: "Occupation — Journalist"), which provides a bridge to the scene of Kane's departure for Europe on a Cunard liner. The assassination material has been condensed in much the same fashion. The scenes showing how Kane's home life suffers as he becomes more deeply involved in the oil scandal story are eliminated. After Kane's encounter with the president, a rapid montage showing cartoon and editorial attacks on the president ends with a close-up of the word *TREASON,* then the assassination itself — a hand firing a gun, hands and uniformed arms struggling with the first hand, the White House in the background, a ticker tape spelling out the news.

The Welles revisions address two of the most glaring dramatic problems in the Victorville material, though still not conclusively. The first involves Emily. While it is possible to eliminate her as a narrator, she is still a necessary presence and force in Kane's life. The story of their marriage has to be accounted for, even if not by her. The Victorville script recognized this by retaining a series of conventional expository scenes chronologically depicting the disintegration of the marriage. Welles threw out the first of these scenes — the couple on their honeymoon — and substituted a much brisker treatment: two brief glimpses of their courtship. In the first, Kane introduces himself to Emily on board a ship bound for Europe and brashly declares his intentions; in the second, a short time later, they are making wedding plans. Welles eliminated a domestic scene that showed Kane doting over his young son but obviously preoccupied with his work and substantially revised a turgid scene after the assassination when Emily makes known her true feelings toward Kane. It is clear that Welles was dissatisfied with the Victorville treatment. In each successive draft of the script, he rewrites the material heavily, until he arrives at a totally appropriate way of playing it — the breakfast table montage.

The second problem involves the surplus of crises in the Leland narration. Most of this section has been rewritten as a kind of extended inquisitorial, in which Leland confronts Kane with the main issues and calls on him for an accounting — his complicity in the assassination attempt, the promotional scheme, his unfairness to Emily, his irresponsibility to others in general. That most of the result is either unfathomable or incoherent is hardly surprising. Welles is simply having Leland do with Kane the same thing *he* was doing with Kane. We do not move very far toward a solution to the problem of crises at this stage. But as a starting point in the necessary process of transforming Kane from Mankiewicz's cardboard portrait into the complex and enigmatic figure we see in the film, this set of revisions has significance well beyond their actual achievement.

Finally, some new material of special interest is added. Georgie, madame of a high-class brothel, makes her first appearance in the story. The party that Kane gives for his staff eventually adjourns to Georgie's Place. On the day of the assassination attempt, Kane is at Georgie's when one of his editors calls with the news. Whether these additions enhance the story or not, Welles himself was very keen on them. The first one remained in the script despite Hays Office objections to it, and although the scenes do not appear in the finished film, they were actually shot (see Appendix). A more durable addition is the lengthy direction that we are to see

Susan's debut a second time, from her point of view — unquestionably one of the most inspired touches in the film.

On June 14, the preliminary budget estimate based on the Victorville script was ready. It showed a total picture cost of $1,082,798 — more than twice the amount specified in Welles's contract as the limit above which special approval was required. It waved another red flag as well: A million dollars was a kind of magic number at RKO. Department heads worked under a standing rule of thumb never to exceed that amount except in the most extraordinary circumstances.[15] In a similar situation, *Heart of Darkness* had been abandoned. Inconceivable as it now seems, the same thing could have happened to *Citizen Kane* even at this late stage. From June 14 to July 2, when the matter was finally resolved, the film was not actually shut down, but its future was definitely in doubt. During that period, the estimate was reduced by more than $300,000. Budgetary realities led to sweeping changes in all areas of the film's production. These areas will be dealt with in successive chapters. Insofar as the scripting is concerned, there were two major consequences: the need for immediate and drastic reductions and the reenlistment of Mankiewicz (because Welles now had to take charge of the overall problem) to assist in accomplishing them.

Welles's initial response was that the changes he had made in the Victorville material had almost surely brought down the cost already. A new draft incorporating all changes was prepared. Before submitting it, he eliminated the sequences set in Rome. Not only did this remove several costly sets from the budget, but it was also a sound decision for the story. The Rome sequences gave us our first view of the adult Kane at a very wrong moment dramatically, where he was living it up in Europe as a young man who had yet to take on any important responsibility. Instead of advancing the story, the Rome sequences tended to slow it down. With this material removed, Kane could now be introduced with one of those sudden and stunning, impulsive strokes that were to become his trademark — just a single sharp line in a letter: "I think it would be fun to run a newspaper." The new draft was the fourth. Called Final (the usual name for the draft first mimeographed), it is the first on which the title *Citizen Kane* appears. It was ready from the stenographic service on June 18. The prognosis of the production estimators was gloomy — "any cuts so far made will not effect major savings," and it is still "fifty to sixty pages longer than the longest script we have ever shot in this studio."[16]

On June 18, Mankiewicz went back on the payroll.[17] He stayed on until July 27, around the time a regular shooting schedule began. During this period, three new drafts of the script were mimeographed. Up until this point, it has been possible to be relatively precise about who wrote what. After June 18, the identification process becomes much more difficult. The problem is not so much that Welles and Mankiewicz are both involved at the same time but rather the unusual production circumstances. Welles was preoccupied with other things now, so we can be sure it was Mankiewicz who was literally making the changes in the script. But to what degree was he determining or even influencing them? During the first week after Mankiewicz's return, the script was reduced by more than twenty-five pages. As

    In the early scripts, the headline proclaiming FRAUD AT POLLS is true: Kane's rivals steal the election, just as Hearst's rivals were widely thought to have stolen an election from him. Later, it was decided that Kane would actually lose after the love nest was exposed. The original headline was kept and made the basis of a comic incident: When KANE ELECTED has to be discarded after the returns become clear, FRAUD AT POLLS is a sour grapes substitute. Welles credits Mankiewicz with the joke. A possible source of inspiration was Fritz Lang's *You Only Live Once* (1937), which contains an incident in which alternate headlines are prepared pending the outcome of a jury verdict.

we shall see, Welles, art director Perry Ferguson, and Gregg Toland jointly managed the budgetary crisis. Did the changes mainly involve adjusting the script to decisions that they had already made? Meanwhile, rehearsals began. To circumvent a rule against uncompensated rehearsing, the cast assembled each day at the Mankiewicz home. How many of the changes came about in rehearsal, with Mankiewicz serving in effect as a transcribing secretary? The records themselves do not provide the answers, but it seems clear that Mankiewicz's creative role was considerably diminished by this time.

    The Revised Final draft, the fifth in all, is dated June 24. There are four principal changes, each one entailing an appreciable reduction in playing time or set costs. A long discussion between Leland and Emily after the election disaster is eliminated. In two other places, the action is telescoped: The early romance of Kane and Emily is now dealt with in a single shot — a closeup of a diamond ring on a hand, from which the camera pulls back to reveal the lovers kissing; the deterioration of the marriage is presented in a single scene; and the dockside scene of Kane's departure for Europe is removed, which eliminates the need for another set.

By July 2, severe cutting in all categories had made possible a revised estimate of $737,740. At this point, Schaefer gave final approval to proceed. One week later, a new draft, the sixth, the Second Revised Final, was ready for the Hays Office. It was fourteen pages shorter than the preceding draft, almost entirely as a result of one fundamental change — the removal of the assassination attempt on the president and its long, talky aftermath. The account of Kane's first meeting with Susan, originally a part of her narration, has been moved to Leland's story to replace the assassination material. In this position, their meeting is followed by the political campaign; now there is only one political crisis to be dealt with. Two of the film's most important conceptions also appear for the first time in this draft. One resolves the problem posed by Kane's first marriage, which has been reduced to the celebrated breakfast table montage: "NOTE: The following scenes cover a period of nine years — and played in the same set with only changes in lighting, special effects outside the window, and wardrobe." The second provides what may be the film's most striking, and is certainly one of its most resonant, images. The previous draft called for an unidentified scene "still being written" after Kane leaves Susan's smashed-up room; it appears in the new draft as the instruction to walk down the corridor between facing mirrors.

The seventh draft, the Third Revised Final — the shooting script — is dated July 16. It contains two very important structural changes. In the preceding draft, the newspaper party had been played in two separate segments — the first half in Bernstein's story, the second in Leland's — and Kane's European trip and engagement had been placed in between. The original justification for this was that the second part of the sequence centered on Leland's objections to Kane's behavior over Cuba. The incident of the opera review was to be broken up in the same way — Leland is found passed out at his typewriter in Bernstein's story; Kane is seen finishing the review in a continuation many pages later — so that each narrator reported only what he could have known firsthand. In the new draft, both sequences are rewritten to be played continuously. This decision smoothes out some rough edges, and it was to have an enormous impact on the effect of these scenes in the film.

THE CONTROVERSY
OVER WRITER CREDIT

Although Welles denies it, the conclusion seems inescapable that he originally intended to take sole credit for the *Citizen Kane* script. The principal evidence is in letters written by Arnold Weissberger, New York attorney for Welles and the Mercury Theatre, to Welles and RKO in September and October 1940. The precedent for such an action had been established on the radio shows. The contractual agreements in radio were similar to those with RKO — Welles, on behalf of the Mercury, signed the primary contract with the sponsor. Writers were engaged under subsidiary contracts with the Mercury, and they assigned all claims of authorship to the corporation. In this way, a legal basis was created for Welles to claim script authorship regardless of the nature or extent of his actual contribution to the writing. He freely asserted the privilege: On the great majority of the radio broadcasts, either Welles was given sole writing credit on the air or no credit was given. Only rarely was another writer mentioned in this connection, and seldom if ever was the writer a member of the regular Mercury Theatre writing staff.[18]

Mankiewicz's contract for work on the *Citizen Kane* script was with the Mercury Theatre, not with RKO. It contained the standard waiver of rights of authorship:

All material composed, submitted, added or interpolated by you under this employment agreement, and all results and proceeds of all services rendered or to be rendered by you under this employment agreement, are now and shall forever be the property of Mercury Productions, Inc., who, for this purpose, shall be deemed the author and creator thereof, you having acted entirely as its employee.

Apparently Welles believed that this agreement gave him unqualified right to decide the *Citizen Kane* scripting credit as he saw fit, as he had done in radio. In Hollywood, however, writers had been able to secure certain countervailing privileges. By industry custom, authorship and screen credit were treated as separate issues. Though a screenwriter signed away all claim to ownership of his work, he could still assert a right to public acknowledgment of his authorship of it. A set of guidelines had been worked out to ensure that those who deserved screen credit got it, and these guidelines were subscribed to by all the major studios. In certain circumstances, a writer who felt unjustly treated could submit his case to arbitration. There were unusual complications surrounding *Citizen Kane*, but the force of accepted practice was strongly in Mankiewicz's favor.

Mankiewicz received his last paycheck on August 3, bringing his total pay for work on *Citizen Kane* to $22,833.35. A letter from Weissberger to Welles on September 6 reveals the course of action they intended to pursue in regard to credits. Weissberger says he has learned that Mankiewicz will probably try to make trouble over the matter of screen credit. He does not want to go into details in writing; an intermediary who is returning to Hollywood soon will explain. He quotes the authorship waiver in Mankiewicz's contract and concludes from it that Mankiewicz has no claim to any credit whatever. He is looking into the situation further, and in the meantime Welles should say nothing. When the time comes, he can confront Mankiewicz with his contract. (Weissberger also explains that he has just learned of possible complications with the Screen Writers' Guild. This and his interpretation of the authorship waiver both indicate how thoroughly unfamiliar he was with the inner workings of Hollywood.)[19] On September 17, the Mercury office drew up a preliminary billing sheet on *Citizen Kane* for review by RKO's legal department. The column for the writer credit contains this curious notation:

"It has not been determined if there is to be a credit given for story or screenplay." This probably indicates that they were following Weissberger's instructions to keep quiet pending further advice. Another possibility is that they were preparing a fallback position in case Weissberger's preliminary opinion failed to hold up: to omit the writer credit altogether, as was sometimes done on the radio scripts. (Better no credit at all than to share credit — that way at least no attention would be drawn.) If so, they were not aware that such a course would have been equally problematic: A request for waiver of screenplay credit would come under a process of review similar to that for credit assignment.

On October 1, Weissberger raised the credits issue in a letter to RKO's West Coast legal department. He begins by repeating his contention that "Mercury's legal right to deny credit can be established." He acknowledges, however, that Mankiewicz may have recourse within the industry, and he asks for details on how similar complaints have been handled in the past. He is particularly concerned, he says, about whether the matter is likely to result in arbitration proceedings and "unpleasant publicity."[20] The reply was guarded but clear in its implications: There are no agreements currently in effect under which Mankiewicz could force an arbitration. A new agreement with the Screen Writers' Guild containing a provision for arbitration has just been executed and will soon go into effect. Since Mercury is not a signatory to this agreement, it is not contractually bound to observe it. Nevertheless, RKO would not want to use this technicality to take advantage of the situation. And, to confirm Weissberger's suspicion, yes, disputes over writer credits generate a lot of publicity.[21]

If Mankiewicz originally had some kind of understanding with Welles on the credits, the course of events can only have made him have second thoughts. As *Citizen Kane* moved along in production, rumors began to leak out that the early footage was sensational. It appeared that what some had predicted might turn out to be true — *Citizen Kane* would be a high point in everyone's career. Mankiewicz began to complain openly. With the general feeling for Welles in Hollywood what it was, support was not hard to line up. In a short time, Mankiewicz was able to build a full-scale word-of-mouth campaign in his behalf. On October 3, *Hollywood Reporter* rated his prospects high: "The writer credit won't be solo for Welles, if Herman Mankiewicz can keep talking."[22] Faced with a combined threat of public exposure and further ostracism from the industry, Welles relented.[23] In a gesture reminiscent of Kane, he put Mankiewicz's name first. The proposed credit read:

ORIGINAL SCREENPLAY
Herman J. Mankiewicz
Orson Welles

When this proposal was submitted to the Screen Writers' Guild for review, an ironic reversal occurred. The Guild pointed out that the credit proposed violated a provision in the writer-producer agreement that a producer could not take screenplay credit "unless he does the screen play writing entirely without the collaboration of any other writer."[24] At this point, Mankiewicz joined Welles in an appeal,[25] whereupon the Guild disclaimed jurisdiction because of the nature of the original contract between Welles and Mankiewicz, and the co-credit was allowed to stand.[26]

Mankiewicz also received a form of public satisfaction. On Academy Awards night, Welles watched in humiliation as *Citizen Kane* lost in category after category and finally won only a shared Oscar for screenwriting. However, that was Mankiewicz's last moment in the limelight. After a temporary upsurge following *Citizen Kane,* his career trailed off again. Welles eventually got vindication of his own. By the time *Citizen Kane* was revived in the 1950s, Mankiewicz's name had been forgotten, along with the dispute over screen credit. Not that the details would have been of much interest: Directors were the prevailing critical interest, and films were being considered strictly as directors' creations. As a result, everyone but Welles was shut out of a share of the newfound glory for *Citizen Kane.* It was against this background that Pauline Kael undertook to rehabilitate Mankiewicz's reputation.

He could not have wished for a more sympathetic biographer. "Raising Kane" is a colorful biography of Mankiewicz as a Dickensian character — a goodhearted loser, undisciplined and always in some kind of hot water, but with a wit that serves as his saving grace. (Consoling his hosts just after he had thrown up on their formal dinner table, he assured them that the white wine had come up with the fish.) It is also a classic piece of journalistic exposé. Kael brought two principal charges: that Welles conspired to deprive Mankiewicz of screen credit and that Mankiewicz wrote the entire script. The second charge made the first seem all the more heinous. Her principal evidence was hearsay testimony from witnesses and participants who were openly sympathetic to Mankiewicz. The first charge seems to be true. Concerning the second, Kael wrote:

> Welles probably made suggestions in his early conversations with Mankiewicz, and since he received copies of the work weekly while it was in progress at Victorville, he may have given advice by phone or letter. Later, he almost certainly made suggestions for cuts that helped Mankiewicz hammer the script into tighter form, and he is known to have made a few changes on the set. But Mrs. Alexander, who took the dictation from Mankiewicz, from the first paragraph to the last, and then, when the first draft was completed and they all went back to Los Angeles, did the secretarial work at Mankiewicz's house on the rewriting and the cuts, and who then handled the script at the studio until after the film was shot, says that Welles didn't write (or dictate) one line of the shooting script of *Citizen Kane.*[27]

This, as we now know, is a flagrant misrepresentation.

Welles attempted a point-by-point rebuttal of Kael in his interviews with Peter Bogdanovich. He also made a brief direct reply in a letter to the editor of the London *Times.*

> The initial ideas for this film and its basic structure were the result of direct collaboration between us; after this we separated and there were two screenplays: one written by Mr. Mankiewicz, in Victorville, and the other, in Beverly Hills, by myself. . . . The final version of the screenplay . . . was drawn from both sources.[28]

Concerning Kael's treatment of the arbitration matter with the Screen Writers' Guild, Welles claims that Mankiewicz's motive was not to guarantee himself co-credit. "Quite the opposite. What he wanted was sole credit." Both Welles's contentions have a degree of factual basis, but each requires careful qualification. There *were* two separate drafts going for a time, as we have seen, but this was *after* Victorville; Mankiewicz's Victorville script was the foundation for all subsequent development. At one point, the arbitration matter did involve a question of sole screenplay credit for Mankiewicz, as we have also seen, but this came along very late, rather than being the issue all along, as Welles implies.

Welles had given a much more accurate summation in his testimony in the Lundberg copyright infringement case. In response to a question about the authorship of a specific scene, he said that it "was written in its first and second draftings exclusively by my colleague Mr. Mankiewicz. I worked on the third draft and participated all along in conversations concerning the structure of the scenes."[29] To summarize: Mankiewicz (with assistance from Houseman and with input from Welles) wrote the first two drafts. His principal contributions were the story frame, a cast of characters, various individual scenes, and a good share of the dialogue. Certain parts were already in close to final form in the Victorville script, in particular the beginning and end, the newsreel, the projection room sequence, the first visit to Susan, and Colorado. Welles added the narrative brilliance — the visual and verbal wit, the stylistic fluidity, and such stunningly original strokes as the newspaper montages and the breakfast table sequence. He also transformed Kane from a cardboard fictionalization of Hearst into a figure of mystery and epic magnificence. *Citizen Kane* is the only major Welles film on which the writing credit is shared. Not coincidentally, it is also the Welles film that has the strongest story, the most fully realized characters, and the most carefully sculpted dialogue. Mankiewicz made the difference. While his efforts may seem plodding next to Welles's flashy touches of genius, they are of fundamental importance nonetheless.

Welles and his cast members begin rehearsals for shooting.

3

Art Direction

Walter Keller had been assigned to *Heart of Darkness* as art director. Keller had worked primarily in theater; *Heart of Darkness* would have been his first major assignment in film. The experience of *Heart of Darkness* made it clear that Welles was going to need someone with more firepower in this crucial position as well as a surer hand. Perry Ferguson was selected for *Citizen Kane*. There are *Citizen Kane* alumni who maintain to this day that assignment to the Welles unit at RKO was a sure mark of studio disfavor. Ferguson's case demonstrates the contrary. At the time, he was the RKO art department's rising star.[1]

Ferguson had come up through the ranks: Originally a staff draftsman, he was made a unit art director in 1935. After a brief apprenticeship in B pictures, he advanced to major assignments. An early credit is for *Winterset*, from the Maxwell Anderson play, which *The RKO Story* calls the studio's "most prestigious 1936 production." He worked with Howard Hawks on *Bringing Up Baby* (1938), RKO's entry in the ranks of major screwball comedies and one of the costliest pictures made by the studio up to its time. In 1939 alone, he received screen credit on three of the studio's top releases, each one in a different story category — *In Name Only*, the year's showcase domestic melodrama; *The Story of Vernon and Irene Castle*, the last of the RKO Rogers–Astaire musicals; and *Gunga Din*, the ultimate escapist adventure and, again according to *RKO Story*, "the most expensive film RKO ever made."[2] A 1940 credit was for *Swiss Family Robinson* (which had narration by Welles), the first in a series of high-quality adaptations of well-known stories.

There is unusual versatility in this list; few art directors are likely to have been involved in so many top-of-the-line productions of such diverse nature over so short a time. According to the standard Hollywood way of thinking, past experience was the surest guide in determining new assignments — hence with Ferguson the recurrence of adaptations, Cary Grant vehicles, and contemporary stories involving sophisticated interior sets. To find the common thread that leads to *Citizen Kane*, however, we must look elsewhere than to the usual genre or story links. On Ferguson's list is a series of textbook examples of troubled productions. Hawks was painstakingly slow and went way over schedule on *Bringing Up Baby*.

Whatever its merits as a film, *Bringing Up Baby* was one of the biggest financial disasters in RKO's history. *Gunga Din* was not far behind. Originally scheduled for Hawks, it was turned over to the usually reliable George Stevens after the *Bringing Up Baby* fiasco, with consequences that surprised everyone. *The Story of Vernon and Irene Castle*, originally intended for Stevens, was then reassigned, but it ran into behind-the-scenes production difficulties on its own and also lost money.[3] Thus, by the time of *Citizen Kane*, Perry Ferguson had emerged as the RKO art department's expert on expensive, high-risk productions involving strongwilled directors. All indications were that *Heart of Darkness* had been headed down the same road as *Bringing Up Baby* and *Gunga Din*. Clearly, what *Citizen Kane* needed was someone with the experience and tact to get along with Welles and at the same time counteract his natural tendency to excess.

Ferguson's former art department colleagues stress two things about him: how fast he was in his work and how well he got along with others. *Citizen Kane* would put his vaunted efficiency to the test perhaps more than any other single assignment of his career. The film had not only an unusually large number of sets, but it also had some very unorthodox set requirements. Yet the financial exigencies were the same as on any other production. Ways had to be found of coping with Welles's sometimes extravagant demands while at the same time observing strict budgetary restraints. The importance of the personal factor also cannot be overstressed. Welles had an uneasy relationship with the RKO professionals. He admired their enormous technical skills, but he found them locked into their own ways of doing things and too often unreceptive to new ideas. Wherever possible, he preferred to recruit his own major talent. On *Citizen Kane*, he brought in his own writer, cinematographer, composer, and even sound specialist. Ferguson was the principal exception. He is the one RKO regular who worked longest, most closely, and most successfully with Welles in a major capacity. One reason they got along was Ferguson's quiet, easygoing temperament. This was crucial, because Welles was painfully self-conscious of his amateur status in Hollywood and hence even touchier than usual. Another was Ferguson's willingness to try new things. In the area of set design, as in other areas, we find bold and groundbreaking new conceptions in *Citizen Kane*.

PRELIMINARY ARTWORK

The next phase after scripting entails the material articulation of what the script envisions. In the Hollywood system, this phase almost always meant the design and construction of complete facsimile spaces on the sound stages rather than shooting in actual locations. A script usually contains only minimal information about the scenes — just the time, place, socioeconomic context, and a few characterizing details. The actual work of physical definition was carried out by specialists in the various departments on the studio back lots. There were four distinct

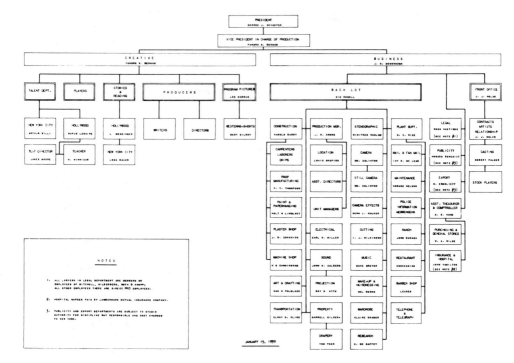

RKO studio organization chart around the time of *Citizen Kane* showing the various departments on the back lot operation.

operations in the process. First, sketch artists would prepare visual treatments of the scenes following the suggestions in the script. After a set of master drawings had been settled on, blueprints would be made and issued to the various construction departments. Bare sets would be built, then painted, papered, and so on. Finally, the set decorators and property people would apply the final touches and ready the sets to appear before the cameras. A designated art director had the general managerial and creative responsibility in this phase. His charge was to come up with an aesthetically valid design plan for the film that achieved the highest possible production value for the price and see to its faithful realization.

On *Citizen Kane*, the official credit reads:

Art Director	Van Nest Polglase
Associate	Perry Ferguson

This billing reflects the bureaucratic prerogatives of the Hollywood system rather than the actual nature of the individual contributions. Polglase was the administrative head of the RKO art department. He read and assigned scripts, attended budget meetings, made art department policy, and generally supervised all the work in progress. But he was rarely involved directly in any major way on the actual work on individual productions. Nevertheless, he was contractually entitled

Welles and Perry Ferguson going over a sketch. Makeup specialist Maurice Seiderman is in the background.

to the principal screen credit for art direction on all RKO films. Working under him were several unit art directors, who were assigned to individual films. Each major production had its own unit art director, and he was usually assigned full-time to that one project. Nevertheless, the unit director received subordinate billing. The technical staff consisted of craftsmen of two principal types: illustrators and draftsmen. The work of the illustrators involved the pictorial elements of the production. They visualized how the sets would look and how the actions taking place in them would be staged. Working from the script, from instructions provided by the unit art director, and from photographs in the studio's research files, they would sketch out the settings and action. The work of the draftsmen involved the building elements — floor plans, layouts, blueprints, and other formal models for the construction of the sets.[4]

On *Citizen Kane,* the specific working procedures were as follows: Welles and Ferguson dealt directly with one another most of the time, not through subordinates. Their work got under way as soon as there was a usable draft of the script. (Ferguson's signed copy of the May 9 script with index tabs indicating the main scenes is in the RKO files.) They discussed each scene at great length. Welles told me he usually did a first set of rough sketches to convey his ideas but found this to be unnecessary working with Ferguson. Ferguson took elaborate notes on their discussions, and the notes became the basis for the instructions given to the illustrators and draftsmen. Ferguson might add an occasional thumbnail sketch involving practical matters, such as layout or prop placement, but the actual visual treatments were done not by him but by the art department staff. He was a specialist in set construction, not an illustrator. As his case demonstrates, to be an art director does not necessarily mean to be a working artist. Ferguson would submit the preliminary sketches to Welles, and the sketches would go back and forth between Welles and the art department until Welles was satisfied. There were two key turning points in this phase of the production. The first was the budgetary crisis in mid May, which has been discussed in the previous chapter. Its impact on the set-planning process was especially severe, and it served as a major challenge to the creative ingenuity of all involved. The second was the arrival of cinematographer Gregg Toland the first week in June. As we shall see, Toland brought a distinctive visual style to the production that had major implications for the set requirements. After his arrival, Welles, Ferguson, and Toland formed a creative nucleus of the production. They met every morning and worked through each sequence of the script, discussing such things as how the sets would look, where the props and furniture would be placed, how the action would be staged, what the camera would be doing, and so on. Together, they worked out a tentative approach to shooting each scene. Establishing such a plan was an absolute precondition for everything else, since the camera range needed for shooting determined how much of a set had to be built. In this way, special set requirements also emerged early — for instance, the need for an unusually large number of "deep sets" on this production (ones with detailing in both foreground and background; in "shallow sets" the background simply trails off) or for special devices or designs to accommodate Welles's and Toland's elaborate camera choreographics and unorthodox shooting angles.

The work of the art department would begin with the drawing of a floor plan based on a proposed shooting approach specified by Ferguson. Then an illustrator would prepare a storyboard (they were called continuity sketches then) visualizing the action. Storyboards were drawn very quickly, and the visual details were very crude (see illustration opposite). The purpose of the storyboards was to illustrate the camera angles that would be needed for the action as envisioned, not to indicate elements of visual design. Because storyboards often correspond closely to the camera setups in completed films, some writing on art directors has tended to treat them simply as evidence of an illustrator's power to determine such things. Actually, the illustrators usually worked to specifications previously determined.

EXT. WINDOW & INT. BED ROOM
KANE'S FLORIDA ESTATE.   (CARD #1.

CAMERA TRAVELS UP TO

WINDOW AND AS WINDOW

FILLS SCREEN-LIGHT

GOES OUT AND WE DISSOLVE

TO INTERIOR —————
(NOTE: SEE OTHER CARD FOR
TREATMENT OF THIS ROOM)

DISSOLVE TO WINTER SCENE

PULL BACK AS DISCLOSE

GLASS BALL IN HAND

WHICH DROPS IT AND

WE FOLLOW BALL AS

IT BOUNCES DOWN STEPS

TS MARBLE

FLOOR WHERE IT

BREAKS AND AS

THINGS QUIET DOWN

PULL BACK TO SHOW

FIGURE IN BED AS

NURSE PULLS SHEET UP

AND WE DISSOLVE OUT.

More creative latitude was used to concretize the details. Typically, the process began with what some called a rough idea — an exploratory sketch in charcoal outlining the main spatial conceptions and the general architectural themes. Its content would be derived from the script, Ferguson's instructions, and actual models, but the composite visual treatment would be the artist's own. A series of variations would be drawn showing different angles of approach or highlighting certain details; other artists would probably prepare alternative treatments of the same material. Ferguson would present the various treatments to Welles, who would approve or reject them in whole or in part and indicate which specific stylistic, decorative, or architectural lines of development he wished further explored.

After a sketch was approved, miniature working models of the sets would be made. Flat, four-sided scale drawings of the furniture and main props would be done on paper, pasted onto cardboard, cut out, and set up. Welles and Toland would work their way through these models with little periscopes, checking how things would probably look and further refining their strategies of object placement, camera movement, and so on. Once everything had been worked out, Ferguson would issue final instructions, and the sketch artists would prepare elaborately detailed working drawings, usually thirty by forty inches, showing each scene as it might appear on the screen. The working drawings would then serve as the master plan and the basis from which construction would proceed. (See illustrations on the facing page, detailing the *Inquirer* exterior.)

Two of Claude Gillingwater's working drawings for *Citizen Kane*. The style is American Ashcan School.

STORYBOARDS AND SKETCHES

Following is a representative selection of the early artwork, with examples of how the sets looked when completed. The sketches are probably by Charles Ohmann, who did most of the early work. An exception is the boardinghouse interior, which has been attributed to Albert Pyke. The storyboards could have been done by anyone. Storyboards were turned out so quickly that they usually lacked individuality, and it was in the nature of things for everybody on the staff to take at least one turn at one thing or another on any given production.

PARLOR

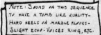
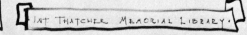

NOTE: SOUND IN THIS SEQUENCE TO HAVE A TOMB LIKE QUALITY - HARD HEELS ON MARBLE FLOORS - SLIGHT ECHO - VOICES RING, ETC.

Int. THATCHER MEMORIAL LIBRARY.

OP. SHOT - STATUE OF THATCHER - CAMERA STARTS TO PAN & TRAVEL

DOWN, SHOWING FULL STATUE - CONTINUES TO ALLOW AUDIENCE TO

READ INSCRIPTION - BERTHA'S HEAD COMES IN AND AS CAMERA PULLS SLIGHTLY BACK WE TIP IN THOMPSON -

BERTHA DELIVERS INSTRUCTIONS TO THOMPSON SAYING "COME WITH ME." SHE

RISES AND STARTS TOWARD DOOR AT REAR FOLLOWED BY THOMPSON AS WE DISSOLVE -

OPENING ON PANEL OF DOOR SEEN IN LAST SHOT - AND DOOR STARTS TO OPEN

REVEALING LIBRARY ROOM AS GUARD IS TAKING MEMOIRS FROM SAFE - CAMERA TRAVELS

THRU DOOR AS BERTHA WATCHES GUARD PLACE BOOK ON TABLE, THOMPSON WALKS FORWARD AND

SEATS HIMSELF - BERTHA'S INSTRUCTIONS CONTINUE AND WE LOSE HER AS WE TRAVEL

FORWARD AND UP OVER THOMPSON'S BACK - HIS SHADOW BRING CATT ON BOOK - WE MOVE

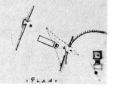

DOWN TILL BOOK CAN BE READ BY AUDIENCE - CAMERA TRAVEL-ING OVER WRITTEN WORDS TILL WE DISSOLVE INTO: HISTORY AS REVEALED BY MEMOIRS -

DISSOLVE BACK INTO SHOT AS BEFORE AND THOMPSON CLOSES BOOK - AS HE STARTS TO RISE CAMERA TRAVELS

FORWARD AND DOWN KEEPING ON THOMPSON'S BACK TILL WE INCLUDE BERTHA AT OPEN DOOR - AT THIS POINT

THEY HAVE THEIR DIALOGUE - IN DISTANCE CAN BE SEEN PAINTING OF THATCHER - WE DISSOLVE TO EXT. OF ENQUIRER"

- PLAN -

"EL RANCHO" CABARET

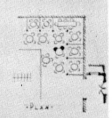

THE EVOLUTION OF A SET

The Hollywood studios usually maintained a complete scripting file on every feature film released. Typically, these files contained the final shooting script and the release continuity, plus copies of such things as the source work on which the film was based, any preparatory materials, such as reader reports, treatments, or synopses, and all intermediate script drafts. This was good business practice. Since the studio usually owned the remake rights, the script file was not merely an archival record: It also represented an actual property with potential additional value. Also, lawsuits involving story rights were common, and full documentation of a script's evolution was often needed as part of a defense. Besides, scripts presented no special archival problems because they could easily be stored in standard-size files. In contrast, a film's artwork was generated in great profusion in formats that were bulky to store, it had no inherent property value, and there was no compelling practical reason to preserve a record of it. Photographs would be taken of representative sketches and drawings, and these would be arranged by subject category and added to the general research files. A few of the original sketches and drawings might be exhibited in the theater lobby for the film's Los Angeles opening. An art department employee might carry off a few pieces as souvenirs or to add to a private file. The great bulk of such materials, however, was discarded or destroyed. As a consequence, it is usually difficult to come by even a reasonably complete record of the art department's work on a typical Hollywood studio feature. Making things worse for RKO is that, when the studio was sold to Desilu Productions in 1957, many of the records and materials (including the art department's) were left behind in order to give the new owners a sense of how the studio operated and to ease the transition.

Fortunately, a small and significant core of the art material for *Citizen Kane* has survived. It is in bits and pieces in all kinds of places, some of them very out of the way. The largest single batch of these materials somehow managed to survive the depredations of the Hughes era and the closing down of the studio. The RKO West Coast business archive contains a set of sixty-eight eight-by-ten-inch matte-finish photographs of storyboards and preliminary set sketches based on early drafts of the script.[5] Altogether, about three-fourths of the sets that appear in the film are represented. (For scenes that do not appear in the film, see the Appendix.) The Mercury collection possesses a few photographs of this type that are not in the RKO files, plus a small number of research photographs (including a series of exterior views of San Simeon). The Museum of Modern Art has a half dozen sketch photographs, the gift of a former RKO art department employee. Other former RKO people have samples of the *Citizen Kane* artwork. Most are photographic copies, but one private collection holds seven original pieces, which probably came from a lobby display.[6] Finally, things can still be found on what was once RKO property. In 1977, the original Rosebud sled turned up in a prop warehouse at Paramount that used to belong to RKO. (Custom-built in the RKO property department, it was thirty-four inches long, made entirely of balsa wood, and fastened together with wood dowels and glue. Actually, three identical sleds were built; two were burned in the filming. The sled is shown on this book's endpapers.) Some of the statues cast for *Citizen Kane* lie abandoned in a warehouse basement at Laird Studios in Culver City, the site of the old RKO–Pathe operation. Little caches of former art department materials turn up here and there in these locations — a filing cabinet of sketch photographs in a closet, a box of set stills in an out-of-the-way corner, a few packing cases of research pictures in an unused warehouse — and occasionally a *Citizen Kane* item is among them. For the most part, this material provides only random and fragmentary glimpses of the creative evolution of the film's physical spaces. In one notable instance, however, there is enough for a relatively full account. Most fortuitously, this instance involves the film's perhaps single most famous set, the Great Hall at Xanadu.

In the story, our first introduction to the Great Hall at Xanadu is when Kane and Susan retire there after her unsuccessful opera tour and suicide attempt. The script provides the following information:

134 CLOSEUP of an enormous jigsaw puzzle. A hand puts in the last piece. CAMERA PULLS BACK revealing puzzle spread out on the floor. Susan (38) is on the floor before the puzzle. Kane (60) is in an easy chair. Behind them towers the massive renaissance fireplace. Baroque candelabra illuminates [*sic*] the scene.

Later, when the reporters assemble in the Great Hall as they are about to leave, a few additional details are given:

161 The magnificent tapestries, candelabra, etc., are still there, but now several large packing cases are piled against the walls, some broken open, some shut and a number of objects, great and small, are piled pell-mell all over the place. Furniture, statues, paintings, bric-a-brac — things of obviously enormous value are standing beside a kitchen stove, an old rocking chair and other junk, among which is also an old sled.

Somewhere in the back, one of the vast Gothic windows of the hall is open and a light wind blows through, rustling papers.[7]

A sketch artist's job, as one of those who worked on *Citizen Kane* explained it to me, was to fill out the suggestions in the script with architectural and decorative designs and combinations that were appropriate to the character and action. It did not require much penetration, particularly for a native of Southern California, to recognize that Xanadu parodied Hearst and his life-style at San Simeon. (Mankiewicz's juxtaposition of Renaissance and Gothic strongly suggests San Simeon, as does the fireplace itself.) Curiously, almost no one I talked to who worked on the film had ever been a guest or even visited there. What knowledge they had of it was based on secondary accounts and on photographs in books. For a sketch artist in 1941 an unmistakable starting point would have been a copiously

illustrated 1931 *Fortune* magazine feature article on life at San Simeon titled "Hearst at Home." Above is a photograph from that article of the Great Hall at San Simeon.

Several details will be precisely echoed in the Great Hall of the film — the massive oak table in the center, a highbacked upholstered armchair beside it, an enormous fireplace in the background. There is also the general sense of clutter.[8] Yet for all the similarity in individual details, the two structures do not look anywhere near the same. One obvious reason is that the sketch artist would have been careful to obscure his original source, for legal protection if nothing else. But a more basic reason is that the Xanadu Great Hall evolved not in simulation of Hearst but according to the dynamics of the script and the exigencies of the production process.

From its earliest conception (above), the Xanadu Great Hall is treated not like Hearst's but as a much larger, more imposing, above all monumental space. The overall idea would have originated in Ferguson's conferences with Welles. For the visual rendition, the sketch artists would have started by combing the research photographs for ideas. The RKO art department maintained elaborate files for this purpose, with representations of every conceivable period, geography, and style. Files would be included not only for larger architectural categories, such as "Palaces — Italian Renaissance" or "Houses — Spanish Colonial," but also for small parts and details, such as gates, arches, fireplaces, and windows. The art department also had its own reference library, which contained several dozen standard works of art and architectural history. When accuracy or historical fidelity was the aim, the files would provide precise models. When the architecture was to be used evocatively, as it was in so much of *Citizen Kane*, the files would provide familiar visual prototypes as a starting point, and the illustrator would improvise the rest.

A key term in the script is *Renaissance*. The RKO art department library contained a standard work, *The Architecture of the Renaissance in Italy*, by William J. Anderson. In this volume was the drawing opposite of an Italian Renaissance forecourt and staircase:

This drawing may be the original visual model for the preliminary sketch. The overall use of space is very similar. As for the architectural details, both structures have an imposing forecourt, a staircase rising to a loggia with vaulted ceilings in the upper level, and figures drawn in on the staircases to give a sense of scale. More tellingly, except for the reversal of direction, the point of view in the two sketches is virtually identical.[9]

Typically, however, the sketch artist has made changes in order to emphasize certain points. Left-to-right composition is more cinematic for the subject matter. The Hearstian element is brought out in the almost perverse juxtaposition of incongruent architectural styles and motifs — Gothic along the far wall, Venetian Baroque in the loggia, Egyptian on the landing (including a sphinx on a plinth!), vaguely Far Eastern figures along the staircase. (Each of these details might have had its original visual model, or they might have been drawn from memory — it probably depended on which would have been faster.) Also, the sense of scale is altered: The staircase in the original drawing complements the human figure, while the staircase in the sketch engulfs it.

A detail sketch of the staircase (below) is even more blatantly thematic. The image is a visual summary of the script: A massive stone staircase leads up to a monument. In climbing, one passes the disparate jumble of a lifetime devoted to

possessing. At the top stands a sphinx, the symbol of an eternal mystery — Charles Foster Kane. As real architecture, this arrangement of elements would make no sense — for instance, the stairs continue beyond the monument to lead finally, it appears, to nothing but a wall of windows in the loggia. But there is no real reason why it should, since the artist's aim is not to make architecture but to appropriate architectural elements in the service of storytelling. Moreover, he does so within a set of visual conventions that would have been very familiar to the filmgoing audience — the Griffith–DeMille genre of spectacle, in which massive, overscaled structures overdecorated with the visual clichés of various historical periods and styles (usually incongruously juxtaposed) signify imperial grandeur, epic scope, non-Aryan mystery, and the lure of the forbidden. In fact, two different architecture historians to whom I went for possible historical models for the sketches both drew parallels not with architecture but with the movies — one to DeMille, the other to the Babylon set for *Intolerance*. The *o.k.* notation on the staircase sketch by Freddie Fleck, one of the assistant directors, indicates that Welles himself liked this line of treatment and was directing that it be followed up. By the time it appears on the screen, however, the Xanadu Great Hall has been purged of most of its elements of standard cinematic spectacle. The explanation probably lies less in aesthetic considerations than in practical realities.

These first sketches of the Great Hall were drawn before budgeting began. When the budget estimate came in, Welles and Ferguson were forced to scale down their plans drastically. A good deal of the scaling down was accomplished in the customary fashion — by making use of preexisting sets and materials and by eliminating scene setups called for in the script. But they also came up with a number of much more innovative solutions. A particularly ingenious combination of these can be seen in what happens to the Great Hall set.

The dramatic requirements of the Great Hall set made Perry Ferguson's job even more difficult. Neither he nor any other of the *Citizen Kane* principals would have been in on the early budgeting sessions, which would have been attended by the department heads (principally Polglase, Darrell Silvera of property, and Vernon Walker of special effects) and the professional budget estimators. In these preliminary sessions, the Great Hall was budgeted as part live action and part a series of "hanging miniatures." The hanging miniature was a photographic special effects process used mainly for large structures, in which a miniature representing a portion of the set was placed between the camera and the part of the set actually constructed. It saved construction costs, but it was enormously inhibiting, because it required precision matching in long shot by a stationary camera. Toland and Welles would be opposed to such a treatment, because it would be at odds with the elaborate camera choreography they preferred. Also, they must have sensed the enormous dramatic potential of the vast empty spaces of the Great Hall set for deep-focus compositions. Consequently, the miniature process would have to be scrapped, and a full set would have to be constructed.[10] The problem for Ferguson, then, was compounded — how to cut costs drastically while at the same time adopting a plan far more costly than the one originally proposed.

Another decision made under budgetary pressure produced important changes in the dramatic requirements of the Great Hall set. The most effective way of lowering set costs was to eliminate whole sets. This could be accomplished either by dispensing with all the scenes called for on a particular set or by relocating them to other sets. In the early scripts, some of the scenes involving just Kane and Susan at Xanadu took place in a living room. (See the Appendix for a sketch.) The Great Hall was intended to serve as a combined social and ceremonial center-piece, just as the Great Hall at San Simeon was. In response to the budget crisis, the smaller, private space was eliminated, and its scenes were shifted to the Great Hall. The consequences were extraordinary, as we shall see.

Claude Gillingwater, Jr.'s later working drawing of the set (below) gives us glimpses of some of the changes in progress. The most dramatic change involves the staircase, which has become much less prominent. This is partly the result of practical necessity. By a fortunate coincidence, it was discovered that a large stair-

case built for another film was still standing on the stage where the Great Hall set was to be constructed. It could be used at a considerable savings, though the enormous sense of scale conveyed by the original staircase design would have to be sacrificed. Again, the visual prototype for the revised plan may have come from Anderson's *Architecture of the Renaissance in Italy:*

The angle of view toward the staircase, its directional placement, and in particular the window lighting suggest the parallel, though Gillingwater's rendition is a
typical outrageous fusion of diverse architectural styles. In this new treatment, the
sphinx is redundant. Almost as if in acknowledgment of the fact, it has been
moved aside and toward the background. Eventually it will disappear altogether,
along with most of the other costly detailing on the upper level.[11]

As the staircase recedes in compositional importance in Gillingwater's drawing, so the fireplace rises to prominence as the set's central feature. Again, this is
appropriate, since elimination of the other set left it the focal point of several key
scenes. Like the Great Hall generally, the fireplace has its origins in San Simeon.
Below is the photograph of the refectory, called the Great Dining Hall, at San
Simeon that appeared in the *Fortune* article. The carved stone chimneypiece in
the background is a French Gothic original that is thought to have come from the
collection of architect Stanford White. The mantel, eleven feet eight inches in
height, is the tallest at San Simeon. The inset figures on the overmantel are Visi-
goth kings.

The preliminary sketch for the chimneypiece at Xanadu (above) is almost a literal rendering of it. Typically, the sketch artist has improvised an extraneous feature: an arched lintel in the English Gothic Revival style. (A good example that could have served as the artist's source is Plate I in L. A. Shuffrey's *The English Fireplace*, London, 1912.) Gillingwater's fireplace retains all the essential features of the earlier sketch, but he has changed enough details to obscure the direct link with Hearst.

In its major details and their placement, the lower half of the Gillingwater sketch is very close to what we see on the screen. Yet in some ways the finished set is as different from the Gillingwater drawing as it is from the Great Hall at San Simeon. These changes came about during the process of constructing the actual set.

Start with the foremost element, the fireplace. The overmantel has been eliminated — undoubtedly to cut costs, but it would have been out of camera range most
of the time anyway. The mantel itself has been so widened that it looks almost as
much like a proscenium arch as like a fireplace treatment. In fact, several scenes
are played as if it were. The mantel would have been produced in the RKO plaster
shop, which employed a permanent staff of plaster casters and sculptors under the
supervision of longtime foreman Joe Zokovich. So large a piece would have had to
be cast in several separate sections, which would then have to be matched and
bonded together. The sculptors would have come up with ideas for the detailing and
submitted them to Ferguson. For the most part, detailing consists of standard orna-
mental motifs, such as rosettes and fleurs-de-lis, but there is one genuine curiosity:
Along the lintel arch is a nautical treatment consisting of a piece of driftwood with
seashells and winding rope. This motif is probably intended to refer to Xanadu's
location on the Florida seacoast. A famous sculptural prototype would be Benjamin
Latrobe's use of native American cornstalks and tobacco leaves on classical
columns in the Capitol Building. Of course, this sort of thing became a cliché in
American estate architecture.

The theme of outrageous juxtaposition is carried out in the props and set deco-
ration. If the statuary flanking the fireplace is clearly in the classical idiom, the
figure on the mantelpiece is just as clearly medieval Gothic. Both figures are
probably copies of well-known originals: The figure on the right might be a Her-

cules of the Farnese type, while the equestrian figure suggests the famous Bamberg Rider in the cathedral at Bamberg, Germany. Such copies were turned out in abundance in Europe, where there was always a market for them among wealthy Americans. Hollywood property vaults also contained a generous supply of them. (However, the female figure was probably cast in the RKO plaster shop. There is a tiny model of her on a table in Susan's second apartment.) Around Susan at the

fireplace is an even more illogical grouping — the classical figure, a bellows from an English country estate, and an ecclesiastical candle bearer that is probably French in origin.[12]

The set as a whole is also very different from the artistic plan. The major change involves the amount of detailing. The Gillingwater drawing envisions a fully illuminated three-sided set with all the spaces filled in. The completed set is selectively illuminated, and whole areas are left dark. This fundamental change represents the difference between visual illustration and the dynamics of set design. Ferguson's problem was to preserve a sense of monumental scale for this set while at the same time significantly reducing its cost. His solution was extremely ingenious. Only the most prominent features of the set were actually built from scratch — the fireplace and the doorway treatment to the left of it. The staircase, we know, was modified from an existing set. The property vaults turned up other pieces that could be used without cost, such as the enormous Gothic entryway at the left of the stairs. The walls were left bare except for occasional hangings and ornaments, but low illumination and strategic placement of statuary and other props helped to camouflage this. Rolls of black velvet were hung in the empty spaces, causing them to register photographically as extreme depth. The result is a very sophisticated piece of optical trickery: The eye continually reads more than it actually sees.

On the screen, the scale, the exaggerated depth perspective, and the lighting plan all work together to give the Great Hall set a powerful sense of the vast and foreboding. Yet the individual parts of the set make possible a more subtle range of effects. The arrangement of statuary here differs from that shown in the set photographs: Here a medieval gargoyle partially obscures the Hercules and looms menacingly toward a neoclassical female figure — a visual pun for Kane's treatment of Susan, and probably a Wellesian touch (see frame enlargement on page 64). More significantly, the fireplace area is made to serve as a kind of living room. The Kanes play out their private domestic scenes in what was obviously conceived of as an enormous ceremonial and display space. The verbal substance of the conventional is there ("Our home is *here*, Susan"), but the surroundings are totally out of kilter. The domestic hearth is more than twenty-five feet long; Kane traverses perhaps twenty yards to get to his favorite chair; their dialogue drifts back and forth across the great empty spaces between them. Except for Susan's puzzles, there is absolutely nothing of a personal or intimate nature around. As we know, these circumstances were dictated by practical necessity, but the dramatic result is to create one of the most startling and psychologically upsetting effects in the entire film.

THE LEGACY

The revised budget of June 27 listed a total of 81 sets for *Citizen Kane,* not counting pickups and inserts.[13] When the film was in production, *Hollywood Reporter* carried a news item stating that it would require a "record number of 93 sets."[14] The souvenir program issued at the time of the film's release quoted Ferguson as saying there were either 106 or 116 sets, depending on how one counted, and that his highest previous count on a film was 65.[15] The fact that this information was deemed newsworthy is in itself an indication of how special the set requirements for this film were. First of all, the number of individual sets was unusually large. Second, these represented a great diversity of places and kinds of settings covering a seventy-five-year period. Next, the deep-focus shooting style necessitated costly foreground and background detailing on many sets. A number of sets had other unusual requirements — muslin ceilings, for instance, or camera boxes built into the floor for low-angle shots. Finally, there were the virtuoso sets specially designed to accommodate Welles's flair for the sensationally dramatic. The Great Hall is merely the flashiest of these. There is also the nightclub sign, a live action set (not a miniature, as most people think) built in halves so that it can fold outward as the camera passes through. Or the interior of Mrs. Kane's boarding house, a small, fully appointed space that the camera can traverse with ease because the walls fold down and the furniture is set into place as the camera truck clears the path. Or the room where the newspaper party is held, an enormous structure with muslin ceilings built on an elevated platform that is large enough to contain, simultaneously, each in its own space, a banquet, a marching band, a chorus line, an emcee, a private conversation, and a cavorting newspaper publisher. Yet all this was accomplished at a cost considerably lower than the average for the time. In the preliminary estimate, $105,575 of the $1,082,798 total had been budgeted for set costs, roughly the 10 percent considered standard for A-type productions. As a result of severe cutting during the budget crisis, the estimate was reduced to $58,775, slightly more than 8 percent of the $723,800 budget. (It is significant that, in the July 2 go-ahead estimate, the total budget had been reduced by 33 percent, but the sets budget had been reduced by 45 percent.) The actual cost ran to $59,207 — within $500 of the estimate and an astonishingly low 7 percent of the total picture cost of $839,727.

Shortly before the film's release, Welles wrote a long letter to Schaefer summing up his experience on *Citizen Kane* and looking ahead to his next project. One of his major achievements, he says, is that *Citizen Kane* looks like it cost a lot more than it actually did. The root explanation, he goes on, is in the art direction — his own careful attention to this phase of the production and the art department's full cooperation in giving him exactly what he wanted. He says he has already asked for Ferguson for his new project and wants him in New York right away so they can start to work.[16] Schaefer did his part to help things along, and Ferguson was assigned for a time to Welles's Mexican story (see Chapter Six).[17] Welles would also have wanted Ferguson for *The Magnificent Ambersons,* but by that time he had left RKO, first to do *The Outlaw* for Howard Hughes, then to become a permanent fixture at Samuel Goldwyn, where he eventually became head of the Goldwyn art department. At Goldwyn, he and Toland formed a team — on *Ball of Fire* (1942), *The Best Years of Our Lives, The Kid from Brooklyn, The Bishop's Wife* (all 1946), and *A Song Is Born* (1948). He worked again with Welles on *The Stranger* (1946), whose few distinctions include a church tower said to be the tallest set built in Hollywood since *Intolerance.* Another notable credit is *Rope* (1948), Hitchcock's experimental single-set, single-take curiosity piece. In the 1950s, he moved over to television, where he is best known for his work on the series "77 Sunset Strip."[18]

Citizen Kane has always represented different things to different people. For Hollywood set designers of the 1940s, it was a textbook example of how to function creatively under severe budgetary restraints. That lesson had special relevance for the times. Only a few months after *Citizen Kane* was released, the war broke out. Among the wartime restrictions that hit Hollywood was a ceiling on the amount that could be spent on new materials for set construction on any one production — a paltry $5,000. In a trade article on this subject published in 1942, Ferguson pointed out how Welles's film could serve as a model:

> There is another way in which we can effectively minimize actual set-construction to great advantage. This is in taking advantage of the camera's powers of suggestion. . . . Very often — as in that much-discussed "Xanadu" set in *Citizen Kane* — we can make a fore-

ground piece, a background piece, and imaginative lighting suggest a great deal more on the screen than actually exists on the stage.[19]

Probably the single most ingenious device was the black velvet technique, which was used not just on the Great Hall set but in other situations that had similar lighting. A leading art director told me he first learned this trick from Perry Ferguson on *Citizen Kane* and that thereafter it became a standard feature of his own repertory. Film history has traditionally assigned credit for the expressionistic lighting of the Great Hall and other sets almost exclusively to Toland. Actually, as we have seen, the lighting program originates in the design of the sets. This is not to deny that Ferguson and Toland may have worked these things out together with Welles. But at the very least, the credit will have to be shared.

4

Cinematography

Welles says it was Toland who first broke the ice. Welles had made it known that he was interested in working with the veteran cinematographer. When word of this reached Toland, he telephoned Welles at the Mercury Theatre office and offered to sign on. After a long string of directors who "know everything there is to know," he told Welles, it would be a real pleasure to work with an amateur. What attracted Welles to Toland is clear enough: his long years of experience, the stature of his assignments, a recent Academy Award (after two previous nominations) for *Wuthering Heights,* and a reputation for unconventionality. He had probably also heard the legend that Toland was "the fastest cameraman alive." What attracted Toland to Welles becomes clearer when we look at the overall contours of Toland's career. Despite the universal professional respect he commanded in Hollywood, Toland was never a creature of the Hollywood studio system. In fact, he was a devoted rebel against the conventions and rituals of big studio filmmaking. His way of escaping them was to work at Samuel Goldwyn Studios, where he stayed under contract throughout his career. At Goldwyn, he enjoyed privileges that would have been less likely to be available in the larger studios: a light production schedule, carefully selected story material, his own specially designed or modified equipment and handpicked crew, an atmosphere conducive to innovation, and the chance to work regularly with nonconformist directors like John Ford, Howard Hawks, and William Wyler, who welcomed and encouraged his innovations. He had access to the Goldwyn facilities between assignments so that he could freely tinker and experiment. His dislike for conventional studio photography was legendary. He was always in the forefront of change, the first to adopt new methods made available by technological developments in lighting, optics, and film stocks. He appears to have been driven by a compulsion to expand the accepted technical boundaries of the medium. He was also a shameless exhibitionist in the films on which he worked, never missing an opportunity for a flamboyant display of whatever new and sensational visual effect he had come up with. He told Welles he had seen and admired the original Mercury Theatre *Julius Caesar,* a more unconventional production than which it would be difficult to imagine. He certainly would

FORM 200 IM 7-38	**SAMUEL GOLDWYN STUDIOS**				
	1041 NORTH FORMOSA AVENUE				
CAMERA NO.	Exhibit "A"			**DATE**	June 4, 1940
1	Mitchell Camera BNC -2				
	Bell & Howell Camera				
1	24 M M Cooke			F 2	228223
	25 M M			F	
1	35 M M Astro			F 2-3	20040
2	40 M M Astro 18890 F 2-3) 813			F 1-3	
1	50 M M Astro			F 2-3	18619
1	75 M M Astro			F 2-3	19548
1	4 Inch Astro			F 2-3	19437
	5 Inch			F	
1	6 Inch Astro			F 2-3	7199
2	Upright Finder and Mattes 708 & 24				
1	Finder Support Bracket				
	Matte Box Complete (Old Type)				
2	Matte Box Complete (New Type) BNC -2 & 24mm special 4 rods				
	Tripod Legs				
	Baby Tripod				
	Straight Head				
1	Freehead Mitchell 7054				
1	Tripod Crank Tripod and points				
4	Camera Crank overhead bases and flags				
1	Speed Motor Crank special dimmer				
	High Hat				
1	Mitchell Motor No 224 (3 sound motors)				
1	Mitchell Motor Case				
	Bell Howell Motor				
	Bell Howell Motor Case				
1	Camera Case				
2	Accessory Case No. 1 & 2				
3	Magazine Case				
	400 Ft. Magazines				
6	1000 Ft. Magazines				
	25 M M Finder Adapter				
1	Measuring Tape 50 ft				
1	128 special diff. screen schiete				
4	N.D. grad 3"x5" Scheibe 25, 50, 75 & 100				
4	Mitchell diff. screens 3"x3"				
3	Grad 3"x5" Scheibe 21, 23A & 23A-56				
47	3"x3" filters glass				
9	disc glass				
2	boxes of 12 filter holders				

List of the equipment Toland brought from Goldwyn for shooting *Citizen Kane*. Toland was the first major cinematographer to use the new blimpless Mitchell camera, the BNC. The 24 mm Cooke was the widest-angle lens in common use at the time.

have known, too, about *Heart of Darkness*. What better proofs could there be that Welles would make an ideal collaborator?

Goldwyn agreed to loan Toland out at $700 per week. As part of the deal, RKO was obliged to employ Toland's regular camera crew and to rent his camera equipment from Goldwyn. The crew, which had worked with Toland off and on since the 1920s, consisted of Bert Shipman, camera operator; W. J. McClellan, gaffer; Ralph Hoge, grip; and Edward Garvin, assistant cameraman. Toland insisted on using his own equipment because some of the pieces were fitted with his own special modifications and also because he was using a camera and lenses that were not commonly used in the major studios at the time. We will consider the specifics in due time. For the moment, we should recognize that, with Toland, Welles was getting more than just a cinematographer on free-lance assignment. He was also unwittingly contracting for the mechanics and apparatus of a specific kind of shooting plan.[1]

Toland reported for work on *Citizen Kane* the first week in June. At the time, the script was still in budgeting. Welles and Ferguson had done some preliminary work, but there was not yet an overall design plan. Once Toland arrived, he, Ferguson, and Welles worked it out in their morning sessions. Afternoons and evenings, Welles spent what time he had left over from working with the actors and revising Mankiewicz's script not only discussing *Citizen Kane* with Toland but also, quite frankly, learning the ropes. Welles says that Toland spent enormous amounts of time patiently explaining the most elementary and basic things about cameras, camera angles, lenses, and lighting to him but that he always did this quietly and in ways that carefully avoided showing Welles up in public. Clearly, too, Toland was selling Welles on the merits of a particular approach.

When the budgetary crisis developed, the RKO front office insisted on holding everything up until it was resolved. Such crises, however, were old hat with the Mercury operation, and Welles was eager to try out some of the things that he and Toland had been discussing. He proceeded with shooting and fabricated a cover story. Because the sets had not been built, it was necessary to improvise. The first day of shooting, Saturday, June 29, 1940, was devoted to the projection room sequence. The budget had called for the construction of a set; a real projection room on the RKO lot was used instead. For the second day of shooting, Thompson's first visit to the nightclub where Susan Alexander sings, a set with a Western background constructed for another production was commandeered. For the third sequence shot, Susan's suicide attempt, only a partial background set was needed because of the lighting requirement. On the daily production reports that were forwarded to the front office, all three days of shooting were listed as "Orson Welles Tests." The tests were the source for one of the colorful legends that has grown up about the making of the film. Robert Wise tells it this way:

> One of the remarkable things about *Citizen Kane* is the way that Orson sneaked the project onto RKO. He told the studio that he was merely shooting tests. . . . After Orson had been shooting for a while, the RKO bosses finally became aware of what he was doing. Then they said, "Okay, go ahead."[2]

Welles and Toland shooting *Citizen Kane.*

As a matter of fact, thanks to the budgeting process, the front office already had
the full script in hand. Welles had other reasons for concealing what he was doing.
When we look at what was actually shot on these three days, we begin to see what
these reasons were.

The first day of shooting: the projection room sequence. This sequence was shot at unusually low light levels. Then the film was "forced-developed" in the laboratory — that is, it was left in the chemicals a longer time than usual to increase the contrast. Forced-developing would ordinarily make the footage unacceptably grainy, but the tonal range in the scene was so high that the grainy effect was minimized.

The RKO projection room used for the first day's shooting was a space approximately thirty by sixteen feet. In this, Welles and Toland placed a camera, equipment, lights, microphones, crews, and nine performers.[3] They shot the sequence at daringly low light levels — only the streams from the projection windows and a few small fill lights. The performers were barely visible, except when they crossed the harsh beams of light. The performances were pure Mercury Theatre — constant overlapping of the dialogue and background voices. The nightclub sequence is filled with equally daring visual conceptions. It opens with an elaborate descending crane shot, the first recorded appearance of the kind of exaggerated moving-camera effects that were to become the Welles trademark. (It was duly accompanied in the production reports by suggestions of profligacy and waste. In the "Reasons for Delay" column was a notation by the assistant director, an RKO company man — "Returned from lunch 1:30 pm and rehearsed and lined up Crane shot to 4:30 pm.") Later on, this crane shot would be joined optically to a similar exterior shot to give the appearance of continuous movement through the skylight. The sequence ends with another extremely unorthodox visual conception. The reporter enters a telephone booth to call his boss in New York. The camera looks into a cross section of the booth. The reporter stands about four feet from the camera. A wide-angle lens is used on the camera to increase the depth. High-contrast lighting is used in the nightclub background to enhance the sense of depth. In the middle distance stand the captain and a waiter. Slumped at the table in the background is Susan Alexander. All three depth planes are in clear focus. The third sequence, the discovery of Susan's suicide attempt, contains the most daring visual conception of all. In the foreground, only inches from the camera, are a medicine bottle and a glass. Behind them, unconscious on the bed, is Susan, sweating and gasping for breath. In the background, Kane and a servant break down the door to get in. All the planes of activity, from extreme foreground to distant background, are in focus.

In its visual appearance, what was shot on these first few days departed radically from the conventions of studio filmmaking at the time. Much of it was openly, blatantly experimental; one member of the camera crew explained later that the whole purpose of this early shooting was to "prove certain new techniques."[4] The one thing as much feared in Hollywood as a runaway budget was radical innovation. If the truth were known, *Citizen Kane* now had both strikes against it. Indeed, Welles had much to hide.

THE CINEMATOGRAPHIC PLAN

In an article on his involvement in *Citizen Kane,* Toland makes a special point of the fact that he came in very early in the film's production. He explains that this was unusual in Hollywood, "where most cinematographers learn of their next assignments only a few days before the scheduled shooting starts." As a consequence, "the photographic approach to *Citizen Kane* was planned and considered long before the first camera turned." The principal elements of that photographic approach are: deep-focus cinematography; long takes; the avoidance of conventional intercutting through such devices as multiplane compositions and camera movement; elaborate camera choreography; lighting that produces a high-contrast tonality; UFA-style expressionism in certain scenes; low-angle camera setups made possible by muslin ceilings on the sets; and an array of striking visual devices, such as composite dissolves, extreme depth of field effects, and shooting directly into lights. Most of these elements ran directly counter to the conventional studio cinematography of the time. As Toland explained, Welles insisted on "letting the Hollywood conventions of movie-making go hang if need be."[5] Toland himself allowed the impression to stand that many of these rules were being broken for the first time in *Citizen Kane.* In fact, most of them had been broken before, by Toland himself, in films on which he had worked for other directors. In a number of its most important visual features, *Citizen Kane* can be seen as a direct and logical extension of Toland's previous work.

It is said that when John Ford was making documentaries for the government in World War II, he could usually tell from the images themselves which cameraman had shot what footage. If we look at Toland's films of the 1930s with *Citizen Kane* in mind, certain stylistic mannerisms seem familiar: the use of reflecting surfaces and multiplane compositions in the Goldwyn musicals; the way Peter Lorre is lighted in *Mad Love;* the corner compositions of a character with his back to us at the side of the frame in *Come and Get It;* Laurence Olivier's face in darkness in some of the scenes in *Wuthering Heights.* Around 1939, however, these similarities begin to be more pervasive. Thanks to major new technical advances, Toland begins to evolve a radically new cinematographic style that develops to its full maturity in *Citizen Kane.*

The first set of advances involves the sharpness of the film image.[6] In the 1930s, the typical studio style tended toward heavily diffused lighting, soft tonality, and a relatively shallow depth of field. This so-called soft studio style can be traced back to the coming of sound, when noisy arc lamps had to be replaced by incandescent lamps, which, though quieter, provided much lower levels of illumination. To compensate for the light that was lost, lenses had to be used at maximum aperture settings; this reduced the depth of field and it could also soften the image. As the decade progressed, technical improvements in lighting and film stocks made possible a return to the sharper, crisper, still-photographic style characteristic of many silent films. But the soft look was still favored, and conservative studio cinematographers usually found it safer to observe established practices than to strike out in new directions.

Several developments made a sharper, deeper, high-contrast image possible. Depth of field can be increased by shooting with a wide-angle lens and narrowing the aperture setting. Among the technical difficulties involved in achieving extreme depth of field are the great loss of light that occurs when the aperture is narrowed and the graininess of the fast film stocks used to compensate for this loss. In the mid 1930s, partly in response to the requirements of the new Technicolor cinematography, a new generation of arc lamps was introduced. They were silent, more controllable, and much more powerful than their predecessors. In 1938, Eastman Kodak introduced its new Super XX film stock, which was four times faster than Super X without any appreciable increase in grain. In 1939, researchers announced the principle of lens coating, which allowed light transmission to be improved by covering the lens surface with a microscopically thin layer of magnesium fluoride. Also in 1939, a new, exceptionally fine-grain stock for release prints was introduced, which virtually eliminated the problem of grain multiplication that appeared when the print passed through successive generations between camera and release.

A second area of technical advance involved the recording instrument itself. In the early 1930s, the standard studio cameras were encased in giant soundproof blimps to eliminate the sound of the camera mechanism. In the mid 1930s, the

Shooting at close range with the BNC.

Mitchell Camera Corporation introduced the self-blimped BNC, which had a built-in noise-dampening device. For understandable reasons, Mitchell chose Toland to test the BNC. (Its first use on a major production is thought to have been on *Wuthering Heights,* for which Toland won his first Academy Award.)[7] The capabilities of this new camera are related to the new optical phenomenon of deep-focus cinematography. As critic André Bazin first pointed out, composition in depth provides the basis for a mode of film narration that is fundamentally different from the older montage style. This newer style he called *realist*—by which he meant its propensity to maintain the continuous spatial integrity of the image through long takes and such devices as moving the camera or staging multiple planes of action in order to eliminate the need for cuts. (In the standard shooting style of the thirties, focus was shallow, and space was fragmented. The visible result on the screen was characterized by the intercutting of partial actions according to regularized patterns within a master scene.) The smaller, more portable BNC permitted a much greater freedom and flexibility of camera choreography than its bulkier predecessors.

Finally, Toland contributed a number of technical innovations of his own. He was known as a "gadgeteer who could make gadgets work for him," and he always had his cameras "loaded with things he had cooked up to aid him in his work."[8] During his most creative period, which extended from *Wuthering Heights* in 1939 to the time when he was drafted for photographic service in the military in the early forties, he invented several processes and devices that were later to come into general use in the industry.

TOLAND AND *THE LONG VOYAGE HOME*

There are striking compositions in depth in *Wuthering Heights* (1939), and *The Grapes of Wrath* (1940) contains both deep-focus compositions and images that approach the high-contrast tonality of documentary still photography. (Almost surely one of Toland's visual models was a photographic feature on real-life migrants in the *Life* magazine of June 5, 1939; it is obvious that some of these photographs were a source for details of characterization and costuming.) However, the first film in which these elements appear as features of a consistent style is Ford's *The Long Voyage Home* (1940), Toland's last film before *Citizen Kane*.

The opening shot of *The Long Voyage Home* boldly announces the visual plan of the film. In the extreme foreground, a native woman propped against a tree

heaves sensuously to the sound of a native chant offscreen. In the middle distance, another native woman is propped against another tree. In the far distance, we see the outline of the steamer that the women will soon visit to bring "companionship" to its restive crew. The scene is in virtual darkness except for shafts of bright light thrown across the profiles of the women and for backlighting on the steamer, which is reflected on the surface of the water. All the depth planes are in focus; the selective lighting of each plane reinforces the perception of depth. This composition is repeated several times in the film, as in the illustration below, where one character listens in on the conversation of a shipmate who is suspected of being an enemy saboteur. The inherent distorting properties of the wide-angle lens function here as an expressionistic element in the composition of this shot.

Throughout the film, objects in sharp focus are made to loom in the foreground between us and the main action, as if Toland cannot resist any opportunity to intrude the cinematographer's presence into the story. In one such shot, a crooked bartender has been caught at his game of shanghaiing drunken sailors, and one of

the crew members punches him: The camera watches from bar level as he reels backward from the blow, sliding along the bar. At the right of the frame, only inches from the camera, is a liquor bottle in focus — a composition that looks forward to the shot in *Citizen Kane* of Jed Leland passed out over his typewriter after he fails to complete his review of Susan's opera debut. In another shot designed to emphasize the depth perspective, the direction of movement is reversed. The camera is almost at floor level; the wide-angle lens takes in an entire aisle of the deck; props along both sides emphasize the perspective; in the extreme foreground are a ladder and a chain, both laid out on perspective lines running toward the camera from center screen to the sides. An air raid alarm has been sounded; a

character is running from the far end of the deck; midway he slips and, still in sharp focus, slides almost up to the camera.

Like *Mutiny on the Bounty, The Sea Wolf,* and dozens of other stories about life at sea, *The Long Voyage Home* centers on a small group of men thrown together in extremely close quarters for an extended period of time. Unlike most other sea films, however, the overall effect of *The Long Voyage Home* is genuinely claustrophobic. Part of the explanation is obvious: The spatially expansive images that are conventions of the genre, such as the shot of a crew assembled on deck at midday or stock shots of a vessel on the high seas, are absent. But an equally important contribution is Toland's filming plan. The BNC camera allowed him to stage actions in very confined playing areas and to shoot the actors at very close range. Most of the film's scenes are shot on small interior sets. Of special interest for *Citizen Kane* is the set where the men bunk: a small, extremely crowded and cluttered area. At the climax of one of the stories, the men gather there to accuse a shipmate of being a traitor. At a dramatic high point in the action, one of the characters gets up and unscrews an overhead light bulb, which removes the principal source of illumination for the scene. The filming continues at a daringly low level of illumination, with objects and the faces of the men just barely discernible in

the semidarkness — a situation and effect that are strikingly similar to the projection room sequence in *Citizen Kane.*

An opening title in *The Long Voyage Home* is in the spirit of Eugene O'Neill: "With their hates and desires men change the face of the earth, but they cannot change the sea." The unrelenting fatalism of the story material find its perfect embodiment in Toland's expressionistic composition and lighting. The film's final shot provides a good example. The young Swede has been rescued from being shanghaied just in the nick of time, but one of the older sailors was not so lucky. The diminished crew returns to the ship. As one of the crew members kneels on the deck to pray, a dark shadow slowly falls like a curtain over the entire scene.

Traditional film history has it that UFA-style expressionism survived underground as it were in the Hollywood horror film until Welles revitalized it in *Citizen Kane.* As *The Long Voyage Home* demonstrates, that version of the story is seriously incomplete. A number of expressionistic compositions in the Ford film are even more precise forerunners of what will appear in *Citizen Kane.* One is a shot with characters spotlighted partly in and out of darkness, as Charles Foster Kane will appear in several scenes. Another is a shot with streams of light falling into a dark

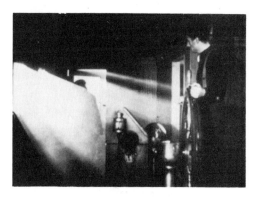

interior, as in the projection room sequence. Another shot uses a reflected surface to create simultaneous action and reaction in the image, as in the sequence of the publisher's party.

Other stylistic traits traditionally associated with *Citizen Kane* also appear in *The Long Voyage Home*. One of these is the extensive use of muslin ceilings on sets. Welles said he originally got the idea for them from Ford's *Stagecoach*, but they are also a regular feature of films shot by Toland during this period, since they are in evidence not only in *The Long Voyage Home* and *Citizen Kane* but also in *Ball of Fire* (1941, directed by Hawks, art director Perry Ferguson). Toland had good reason for encouraging their use: Not only did they permit shooting and lighting from below, unorthodox devices of which he was fond, but they also eliminated the shadows that would be thrown by boom microphones directly overhead, thus increasing the camera's operative range and mobility.

Another Toland device is shooting directly into lights. This was not an acceptable practice in conventional cinematography of the time because of the extraneous halo effect that appeared in the photographic image. The halo effect was caused when direct light rays bounced off the surface of the metal iris back onto the front element of the lens. Toland had been able to eliminate this unwanted effect with a device that he may have used first on *The Long Voyage Home*. He removed the regular sliding aperture from the lens and replaced it with a special insert that would hold a device used in still photography — the Waterhouse stop, a black plate with a round hole corresponding to the appropriate f-stop and serrations around the outside edge of the hole that cut down the reflections and thus eliminated the glare. It gave just the kind of flashy dramatic effect that Welles desired, but it also had some very practical applications. For instance, shooting into the bank of stage lights for the second telling of Susan's opera debut eliminated the need for a costly background audience.

WELLES AND TOLAND

On *Citizen Kane*, Welles not only encouraged Toland to experiment and tinker, he positively insisted on it. As we have seen, from the first days of shooting, they approached the film together in a spirit of revolutionary fervor. This atmosphere continued to characterize their relationship throughout the production. Those involved say there was a kind of running game between the two, with Welles coming up with one farfetched idea after another and challenging Toland to produce it and Toland delivering and then challenging Welles to ask for something he could not produce. Some of the devices Toland came up with he had already used in other films, but others were new or used in significantly new ways in *Citizen Kane*. One example is the distorted image of the nurse who enters Kane's death room. For this shot, Welles wanted a surreal effect, as if the camera were actually seeing through one of the broken pieces of glass. To accomplish this, Toland fitted the camera with one of his gadgets. He placed a diminishing glass (that is, a viewing device that produces the optical effect of looking through the wrong end of a telescope) a short distance in front of his wide-angle lens. The result is a forerunner of the extreme wide-angle fish-eye lens that came into general use in the 1960s.

A whole range of examples of Toland's ingenuity can be seen in the various in-camera effects he devised for *Citizen Kane*. In some, he was pursuing a visual course that had become more or less outmoded. Between 1932 and 1940, the art of optically printed special effects first came into its own. RKO was one of the leading studios in that field (see Chapter Five). By the end of the decade, the trend was to have as many of a film's special optical needs as possible met in the camera effects department, not in principal photography. Toland continued to insist that special optical effects were the province of the cinematographer and that it was his duty to devise ways of meeting special optical needs. (A primary motive must have been his almost fanatic pride in the sharpness of the image. Optical printing is a duplicating process that progressively degrades image quality.) One such device is the four-part in-camera dissolve that serves as a recurring transitional motif in *Citizen Kane:* The background of a scene fades out, then the characters in the foreground; the background of a new scene fades in, then the new characters. The effect is created by dimming the lights by sections, then bringing them up again the same way on the new set; it is very appropriate to the elegiac and reflective moods of most of the storytellers. Another example occurs at the beginning of the film. As we approach the outside window of Kane's bedroom at Xanadu, the profile of a sheeted figure is visible on the bed inside. The light dims. Suddenly, without a cut, we are inside, but the profile on the bed is in exactly the same place on the screen. The transition is accomplished by means of an in-camera dissolve: The first shot slowly goes dark, the film is rewound to precisely the right point, the setup is reverse matched on an interior set, and the lights are slowly raised again. Dramatically, the effect is a typical piece of Wellesian bravura, but it also carries a self-reflective overtone: The very first appearance on the screen of Welles, who is a practicing magician, is accomplished by a stunning feat of visual magic. (In the same way, the first public line he speaks in the film — "Don't believe everything you hear on the radio" — alludes to the infamous "War of the Worlds" broadcast.) An equally striking example of an in-camera effect has almost never been recognized as one: the shot of the bottle and glass on the nightstand after Susan's suicide attempt.

The multiplane composition revealing Susan's suicide attempt is not an extreme deep-focus effect, as it is usually described, but an in-camera matte shot. First, the foreground was lighted and focused, and shot with the background dark. Then, the foreground was darkened, the background lighted, the lens refocused, the film rewound, and the scene reshot. In a famous analysis, André Bazin showed how a narrative logic of cause and effect is embedded in the composition of this shot. Bazin's point is valid, but his underlying premise was wrong: The shot reveals Welles not as a photographic realist but as a master illusionist.

Exerting such a major influence on a film's visual plan in this way was nothing new for Toland, as we have seen in the case of *The Long Voyage Home*. But Toland himself was the first to recognize the special significance of his work on *Citizen Kane*. In "Realism for *Citizen Kane*," an article which was published several months before the film was released, he wrote:

During recent years a great deal has been said and written about the new technical and artistic possibilities offered by such developments as coated lenses, super-fast films and the use of lower-proportioned and partially ceil[ing]ed sets. Some cinematographers have had, as I did in one or two productions filmed during the past year, opportunities to make a few cautious, tentative experiments with utilizing these technical innovations to produce improved photo-dramatic results. Those of us who have, I am sure, have felt as I did that they were on the track of something really significant, and wished that instead of using them conservatively for a scene here or a sequence there, they could experiment freehandedly with them throughout an entire production.

In the course of my last assignment . . . the opportunity for such large-scale experiment came to me.[9]

While Ford seems to have taken a real fancy to Toland's dark and brooding images in *The Long Voyage Home,* they are strikingly at odds with the folksy humanism that is the real core of the film, and Toland's contribution could be described as a visual plan in search of a theme. In *Citizen Kane,* in contrast, the visual conceptions are more fully integrated with the film's thematics. Toland knew this had come about because he had been in from the beginning and because he and Welles were in almost total agreement on everything. He also thought he had a firm understanding of how the method related to the meaning. The film's keynote, he wrote, was "realism"; his and Welles's guiding motive throughout the production had been to make the audience "feel it was looking at reality, rather than merely at a movie" — hence the ceilings on sets, as if they were real rooms; the depth sense, which was closer to what the eye actually sees; the continuous takes in something resembling real time; and so on. From today's perspective, Toland's analyses are almost comical, as if he had been around Welles almost day and night for six months and never understood that it was the flashiness and potential for showmanship of such techniques that really excited him. This, in fact, was the nexus of their collaboration — the deadpan Toland coming up with one zinger after another just to prove he could, with Welles the showman sensing and realizing their dramatic potential for his story.

Deep-focus cinematography provided Welles not with realism but with the technical means of adapting the Mercury Theatre performance style to the requirements of a new medium. Extreme depth of field gave them a playing space roughly equivalent to what they had on a stage. The wide-angle lens kept them suitably distanced. (There is one very good reason why there are so few close-ups in the film: the heavily theatrical gestures and mannerisms of the Mercury players, Welles included, are very unsuited to the studio style of intercutting.) Long takes permitted them to play scenes almost continuously, as they were accustomed to play them on the stage. The extreme mobility of the camera allowed Welles to exercise fully his special talent for elaborate choreographics.

Sets were built with muslin ceilings and often gave the feel of real rooms, with camera placement limited by the physical surroundings.

The lighting plan also has dramatic relevance to the story material. The technical advances of the late 1930s made two different kinds of developments in lighting possible. On the one hand, it became possible to shoot in full light with high-intensity, point-source arc lighting and produce the crisp, sharp tonality of still photographs. On the other hand, it was also possible to shoot at much lower levels of illumination than before, thereby producing very striking expressionistic compositions. As we have seen, in *The Long Voyage Home* Toland was determined to push both effects to their extreme limits, and he was so successful that the cinematography sometimes displaces the story. The two lighting styles reappear in *Citizen Kane,* but there they are made to serve a clear dramatic and thematic function. The crisp, high-contrast daylight style predominates in the first half of the story after the newsreel — that is, in the parts dealing with Kane's rise to prominence in American life. Here, Kane is seen as a self-starter, an idealist, a reformer, a figure of dynamic energy, a traditional type — the hope of the future embodied in a genuine American titan, the entrepreneur tycoon. A contemporary reviewer remarked of these scenes, "Gregg Toland's photography is magnificent. I think it's modeled after the old, needle-sharp pictures of Eugene Atget."[10] By contrast, most of the harshly expressionistic scenes involve the later part of Kane's story, after he has betrayed his promise and become a petty and ruthless tyrant. Above all, we associate such images with Xanadu, where the symbol of hope has become a figure of defeat — cold, aloof, and alone in his gigantic pleasure palace. The two styles of lighting express the polarity that is central to Kane.

Finally, while in *The Long Voyage Home* Toland's gadgets sometimes seem merely gratuitous (as when the captain at the beginning waves his flashlight into the camera for no particular reason), in *Citizen Kane* the effects are usually worked into the action (when the opera debut is shown from the stage looking into the lights, we see it from Susan's point of view). And the endless flow of daring new visual conceptions and devices is totally appropriate to a film like *Citizen Kane,* which deliberately sets out to rewrite all the rules and conventions according to which films are made.

THE LEGACY

Although principal photography on *Citizen Kane* was completed in late October, Toland stayed on for several weeks to shoot retakes and additional material. In mid November, however, he was recalled by Goldwyn for assignment to Howard Hughes on *The Outlaw.* To ensure the optimum uniformity of visual style in *Citizen Kane,* he arranged for his crew to stay on for an additional two weeks to do wrap-up work under the supervision of RKO cameraman Harry Wild. Their services were concluded on November 30 with (appropriately) the final takes of Kane's death scene. Welles made special recognition of Toland's contributions by putting their names together on the same title card in the film's credits. (Interestingly, Ford had paid Toland the same tribute on *The Long Voyage Home.*) Welles wanted Toland for his Mexican story and apparently got a verbal commitment for him from Samuel Goldwyn,[11] but the project fell through. He also asked for Toland for a proposed American version of *It's All True,*[12] but this arrangement, too, failed to materialize, and they never worked together again. After completing *The Outlaw, Ball of Fire,* and *Little Foxes,* Toland was called into wartime service with Ford's OSS photographic unit. He returned to Hollywood after the war and worked on a half dozen productions before his untimely death, at age forty-four, in 1948.

Toland was nominated for an Academy Award for *Citizen Kane.* He lost out to Arthur Miller for Ford's *How Green Was My Valley* — ironically, an assignment that Toland had been prevented from taking by a lengthy delay on *The Little Foxes.* *Citizen Kane* lost not only for cinematography but in seven other categories as well. With Toland, Wyler, and Ford off to do military service and with Welles washed up after his South American fiasco, the evolution of deep-focus cinematography came to a virtual halt until after the war, when a shift toward realism brought it into the Hollywood mainstream. Toland returned to it in *The Best Years of Our Lives* (1946), in industry wisdom the most prestigious assignment of his career. UFA-style expressionistic lighting, however, came into vogue on Hollywood sets a short time after the release of *Citizen Kane.* One finds such effects in films as diverse as George Cukor's *Gaslight,* Val Lewton's RKO horror pictures,

This Gun for Hire, Mildred Pierce, and a prestigious literary adaptation like *Jane Eyre.* A familiar theme in criticism is that *Citizen Kane* was largely responsible for this trend. For instance, Thomas Schatz in *Hollywood Genres* treats *Citizen Kane* as an archetype of film noir and claims an enormous influence for it on the development of that genre.[13] This seems to me an oversimplification. Likelier explanations for the resurgence of the expressionist style are the wartime restrictions on set costs discussed in Chapter Three or the emergence of European-trained directors, cinematographers, and — especially — art directors in the Hollywood studios after the cream of native talent had been enlisted in the war effort. The Academy's categorical rejection of *Citizen Kane* seems to me a much more accurate reflection of the film's status in Hollywood. George Cukor expressed the prevailing view: "I must say I thought *Citizen Kane,* in spite of its brilliance, was rather too much UFA."[14] A memorial tribute to Toland by his British colleague Douglas Slocombe illustrates how ambivalent and uneasy Toland's peers felt about his achievements in this film:

Gregg Toland's contribution to *Citizen Kane* was obviously considerable and it is indeed difficult (as in so many pictures) to disassociate his work from the picture as a whole. Several years after seeing the film I find that one is inclined to remember the image rather than the message, which suggests that *Kane* might have been a very much better film had the novel technicalities not been allowed to run away with their masters. Technically it was certainly an exciting picture to watch with really powerful compositions and dramatic lighting effects despite a certain "rawness" and lack of texture from which one concludes that Toland had not yet tamed his process to wieldy limits.[15]

5

Postproduction and Release

On October 24, the day after principal photography officially closed, Welles left for a three-week lecture tour through the Southwest and Midwest. Along the way, he stopped in Tucson to scout possible future locations with Ferguson and Toland. His return to the studio on November 12 marks the beginning of the fourth major phase in the making of the film. Four main functions are performed during postproduction: the creation of special effects; the sound re-recording, that is, the mixing or "dubbing" of various kinds of sound onto a single track; the composition, orchestration, and recording of the music score; and the editing. It was common practice in Hollywood for directors to leave such technical matters as these to the experts and accept the outcome. In contrast, Welles became heavily involved in the actual work of postproduction and, predictably, refused to settle for conventional results. As a consequence, postproduction on *Citizen Kane* was extremely creative, and some of the film's most original conceptions came about in this phase.[1]

SPECIAL EFFECTS

Special effects is an umbrella term for a range of devices used to create illusions in the projected image, such as matte painting, models and miniature sets, background projection, mechanical gadgetry, and the compositing of images through optical printing. (A separate category, effects created in the camera during principal photography, is treated in Chapter Four.) There is considerably more special effects work in *Citizen Kane* than in most Hollywood films of the era. One reason is financial. As we know, *Citizen Kane* was made on a budget that, for the nature and scope of its subject, was severely limited, and every effort had to be made to keep costs down. Where the makers of the lavishly produced *Wilson* (1944) could afford to stage a full-scale political rally with hundreds of extras, Welles was forced to resort to optical trickery: In the shots of Madison Square Garden from the audience side, only the speaker's platform is a live action set; the giant hall and the audience are painted in. Light flickering through tiny openings in the surface of the painting suggests the rustling of programs. A simulated movement gives the impression that a camera crane descends into the arena. Reverse shots toward the audience are of tiny details — Emily and Kane Junior in a private box, Leland standing in some distant recess of the hall. A later shot from a balcony is a split screen composite with a single character looking downward printed on half of the image and the arena composite printed on the other. Several of the grander actions in the film are created through such means.

Welles's fondness for dramatic hyperbole is another reason for the profusion of special effects. He became completely caught up in the special effects activity and in fact insisted on dominating it. The best evidence for this is the testimony of those who were directly involved. In a memo to superiors explaining delays in completing its share of the work, the head of the special effects department blamed Welles's intransigence and his habit of coming up with new ideas after the fact. To prove his point, he attached a two-page list of items that had not been called for in the original budget or that had been done over at Welles's insistence three, four, five, and as many as eight times.[2] Most of the examples I discuss here are on that list.

At RKO, unlike other studios, the special effects functions were combined in a single, integrated department called Camera Effects. The department was headed by Vernon Walker, whose specialty was background projection. There were cameras specifically designed or modified for effects shooting. Russell Cully was the special effects cinematographer. Douglas Travers was responsible for montages and other editorially created effects. Mario Larrinaga was the matte artist. Linwood Dunn operated the optical printer. There is very little background projection in the film; this technique ran counter to Welles's love of deep focus and elaborate camera movement. One of the few examples has not always been recognized as such. As we know, Joseph Cotten did his scenes on the hospital roof on short notice after Welles sprained his ankle while shooting. Since there was no set, Cotten performed in front of a blank wall. The background — a series of photographic slides projected onto a translucent screen — was added later. (Another example of a projected background is the ocean seen behind Susan and the screaming cockatoo when she crosses a loggia at Xanadu.) Good examples of special effects cinematography are the extreme close-ups of typewriter keys striking a page and of lips whispering *Rosebud*. Travers's newspaper montages are crisply photographed and full of energy and high spirit. Some of the matte work is exceptionally well done — subtly concealed and skillfully merged with the live action (see illustrations). One painting, the exterior of Xanadu, is extraordinary; it will be discussed below. By far the most important special effects technique used in the film, however, is optical printing.

In the early days, most special effects were the province of the production cinematographer. Before matte paintings came into use, the equivalent effect could be created by placing a miniature or a glass painting on a stand between the camera and the live action part of the set. Fades, dissolves, superimpositions, and compositing effects were made in the production camera. With the emergence of the studio system in the 1920s, special effects developed as a sepa-

The first RKO optical printer, designed and built in the early 1930s by optical printing pioneer Linwood Dunn (shown here) and his assistants, Cecil Love and Bill Leeds.

rate art and professional craft. In the early sound era, the art of optical printing came into its own. An optical printer is a device in which a camera and a projector are lined up facing one another and made to run in exact synchronization. Developed film running through the projector is exposed on raw stock running simultaneously through the camera. By varying the light in the projector, one can create fades. By exposing the camera footage twice, one can make dissolves and superimpositions. Composite effects can be achieved in the camera footage by running separately photographed image components through the projector. The earliest optical printers were Rube Goldberg affairs rigged up in a studio's machine shop to fit the needs of its own special effects department. One of the first optical printers was built by Linwood Dunn at RKO in the early thirties (see illustration). It was the prototype for the first standardized, commercially produced optical printer, the Acme-Dunn, which is still in use in some situations today. Since optical printing is a process of image duplication, some loss of image quality is inevitable. The more complicated the effect, the more duplica-

The *Inquirer* employees get their first glimpse of Kane's fiancée. Only a detail of the set was actually constructed. The building and its surroundings were painted in by the matte artist.

Kane and his guest on a picnic procession to the Everglades. The live action was shot on the beach at Malibu, where the surrounding terrain is hilly. The matte artist painted in a flatter prospect and vegetation more suggestive of a Florida location.

tions and the greater the image degradation. Because of the enormous efficiency of the process, however, the industry was willing to tolerate this side effect, and optical printing came into such widespread use that Dunn himself ventured the assertion in 1934 that "during the past four or five years there has not been a single production released that did not utilize the services of the optical printer to a considerable extent."[3] One of the staunchest holdouts was Gregg Toland, who continued to insist on doing his own effects in the camera long after others had moved away from the practice. When Dunn suggested to him that some of the effects he was laboring over on *Citizen Kane* could be done a lot more easily in the optical printer, Toland's terse reply was that he didn't like dupes in his pictures.[4] Welles himself was much more receptive.

One of the flashiest optically printed devices is the wipe, in which one image supplants another by overcovering it or pushing it aside. The transitional mechanism is usually a visual metaphor. The possibilities are endless. In a trade article on tricks by optical printing, Dunn gave more than twenty different examples from recent RKO productions with accompanying photographs — wipes resembling everything from a page turning in a book to a propeller whirling, bubbles expanding, and a sawing effect. One of the most common variations is the curtain wipe, in which a horizontal bar moves up or down pushing one image out of the frame and revealing another. In *Citizen Kane,* the curtain wipe is used with considerable narrative sophistication. In the opening shot at the Thatcher Library, the statue of Thatcher is a miniature. By a skillfully concealed curtain wipe, we move to the base of the statue, which is an actual set; then the camera pulls back to reveal Thompson engaged in conversation with the archivist. As printed, it appears to be a single continuous shot. Optical trickery achieves the same effect that Welles and Toland were after in the production photography — of elaborate camera virtuosity revealing an unbroken succession of events. An even more complex use of the same device occurs in the first presentation of Susan's opera debut. In what appears to be a single sustained movement by the camera from stage level to high up in the flies, we actually have live action, a curtain wipe to a miniature of the backstage rigging, then another curtain wipe back to live action and the two workmen on a platform.

Other optically printed effects are visually consistent with the cinematographic style. One of Welles's and Toland's favorite deep-focus devices was to place a figure in the far background, as when Bernstein is seen in a doorway as Kane fires Leland and finishes his review. Welles wanted a similar effect later in the film in an action for which there was no set. Dunn produced this image for him in the optical printer.

The shot opposite is a composite made from three separately photographed elements. At the center is Kane, rendered through an image-reduction process known as *miniature projection.* Surrounding it is a matte painting with an extremely realistic detail of Kane's reflection on the floor. The scene is based on a

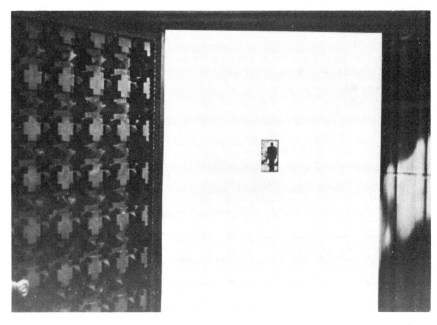

research photo of a perspective in the Alhambra, but the banding on the columns in the foreground is an added Victorian element. At the edge is a prop door, Spanish in style but with a neoclassical jamb — a further elaboration of the incongruent architecture theme.

Welles and Toland were also fond of bringing objects up close to the camera in sharp focus. But there was a limit on how close they could bring the object and still keep it in focus. In the single most important use of extreme close-up in the film, the optical printer was used to achieve an effect not possible with the production camera. The final move up to the decal on the burning sled was accomplished by placing footage of the sled in the optical printer and moving the projector toward the recording camera as the footage ran through, thereby creating an optical zoom effect. There are some even more extreme examples of this device. In postproduction, Welles decided that at certain points he wanted the camera not just to come near objects but actually to seem to move inside or through them. Dunn says that Welles pushed him to achieve this effect in the shot in which Kane on his deathbed looks into the glass globe. The maximum distance the optical printer's projector could be moved toward the camera equaled four magnifications. At that point, the final frame had to be rephotographed and the procedure started over again. By the time he had printed down to the intended effect, the image was grainy and had noticeably lost resolution. Confronted with this result, Dunn says, Welles came up with one of his "inspirations" — superimpose an image of whirling snow over it, and the loss in resolution would scarcely be noticed. A similar invention is used at the point when the camera seems to move through the skylight down into Susan's nightclub. This illusion occurs in the context of an elaborately choreographed production shot in which the camera moves up the side of a building, through a sign, and down to the roof. Dunn took the end of this shot and optically printed it to move into the skylight. The continuation was a crane shot moving down into the nightclub. Dunn took the beginning of this shot, made a reverse optical zoom from it, and printed the result in forward motion. Where the two optical zooms joined, the camera seemed to pass through the glass. To distract the eye from the mechanics of the trickery, he printed in a flash of lightning at this point.

A different category of effects is used in the opening Xanadu sequence. The approach to Xanadu begins with a moving camera shot up a prop fence, and it continues with a series of shots, connected by fades and dissolves, of miniatures, models, and background paintings. Ordinarily, the unreality of these shots might be too distractingly obvious, but the trancelike and surreal atmosphere of the sequence confers on them a fantasy reality of their own. The most visually compelling of these images is the castle itself. The exterior of Xanadu is a background painting. The original would have been painted on a sheet of glass approximately three by four feet. It would be the master from which a whole series of paintings showing Xanadu from various angles and distances and at various stages of completion was prepared.

According to Higham, former Walt Disney artists were involved in the work, and the visual prototype of Xanadu is the castle in *Snow White and the Seven Dwarfs*.[5] Welles denies the link. John Mansbridge, present head of the Disney art department, who was a draftsman in the RKO art department in 1940, seconds Welles and says that the Xanadu painting is the work of matte artist Mario Larrinaga.[6] There is another, much more likely architectural source. The original starting point was probably San Simeon.

Above is one of a series of photographs of San Simeon in the Mercury Theatre files. For each of the photographs, there is a corresponding painting in the film showing Xanadu in a similar placement. However, the main visual themes probably come from an even more famous source, Mont-Saint-Michel (below).

Xanadu and Mont-Saint-Michel are alike in their positioning at the crest of a promontory, in their architectural mass, in their central vertical thrust, and in the proliferation of functional spaces along their exteriors. The Mont at sunset is a familiar visual theme, and in this aspect (although this is not evident from the photograph shown here) the light through the central tower stands out dramatically against the darkness of the surrounding edifice.

In contrast, the individual architectural details of Xanadu are distinct and for the most part unrelated to one another. Each detail can probably be traced to a familiar historical prototype. Like the sketch artists, Larrinaga would have gone to standard architectural sources for precise models. To give a few likely or possible examples: The tower to the farthest right suggests the campanile of San Marco in Venice as it is shown in Anderson's *The Architecture of the Renaissance in Italy* (see Chapter Three and illustration below). The arched colonnade directly below it in the Xanadu background painting suggests a detail of the Palazzo Pitti in Florence as it is given in the same source (see illustration on next page).

To the left of the Xanadu colonnade is an arched entryway in the Victorian Gothic
style, a feature that can be found in, for instance, All Saints Church in London. To
the left of the arch, at the same level, is a Gothic feature, a rosette cathedral
window. Clockwise from there around the perimeter are machicolations such as
would be found on a medieval fortress, another Italian tower, a more massive
tower perhaps along the lines of the Giralda in Seville, and a roof treatment reminiscent of a nineteenth-century German castle.

   This is not to suggest that we would be able to sort out these intricacies when
watching the film. Although the exterior of Xanadu appears numerous times, the
shots are always brief, and the castle itself is always remote in the image. However, we cannot fail to sense the extreme visual incongruity — the same sort of
experience we are supposed to have when we look at the Babylon set in *Intolerance*. Of course, the original inspiration for the concept was Hearst and what he
had done at San Simeon. But there is much more to the painting than this simple
idea. In visual terms, Xanadu is a compositional contradiction. On the one hand,
there is a strongly unified sense overall — it is literally an image of a monument
and literally a monumental image. On the other hand, the individual elements not
only fail to cohere, but they are radically incompatible. In short, Xanadu is what
the film says its protagonist is — distant, remote, inaccessible, a romantic image of
a unified whole, but at the same time possibly no more than an empty parade of
stylistic flourishes and gestures. The theme of a physical structure that reflects its

principal inhabitant is common in literature and films as well as in architecture, and there is enough of it in the film that we know it was constantly on Welles's mind. However, the precise visual solution embodied in the background painting of Xanadu is the contribution of the artist in special effects.

If shooting a film was like playing with a giant toy train set, as Welles once maintained, special effects must have seemed to him a veritable magician's bag of tricks. One informed estimate is that more than 50 percent of the film's total footage involves special effects of one kind or another.[7] Dunn says that in some reels the percentage of optically printed work is as high as 80 percent. So much of this is so artfully done, however, that even the most sophisticated viewer can miss it. A cliché of film criticism since André Bazin is that *Citizen Kane* is a, if not the, supreme example of photographic realism. It seems to me more to the point to recognize the film for the masterpiece of subtle illusionism that it is. In a sense, it is a kind of ultimate realization of Welles's magic act.

SOUND

Of all directors who have worked in Hollywood, Welles has the firmest grasp of the dramatic properties of sound. He had mastered that aspect of his art through years of experience in radio. Before Hollywood, his career moved along two parallel tracks. He was an actor and director on the legitimate stage who supported himself by means of radio work. When he was appearing in his first Shakespearean roles on Broadway, he was moonlighting as an actor on the "March of Time" radio series. As his stage reputation grew, he was also becoming prominent as a result of his radio activities. His best-known performance before "War of the Worlds" was not in a play but in the part of the radio announcer in Archibald Macleish's radio drama "The Fall of the City" (1937). Even before the first Mercury stage production, there had been an ambitious seven-part Mercury radio adaptation of Victor Hugo's *Les Misérables*. It was the "War of the Worlds" broadcast that made Welles a national name, brought him a lucrative contract for a regular series, and made him irresistibly attractive to Hollywood. Even while *Citizen Kane* was in production, Welles and the Mercury people continued to do the weekly radio show.

Welles's background in radio was one of the major influences on *Citizen Kane.* Some of the influence is of a very obvious nature — the repertory approach, for instance, in which roles are created for specific performers with their wonderfully expressive voices in mind. It can also be seen in the exaggerated sound effects. The radio shows alternated between prestigious literary classics and popular melodrama. Welles had a special fondness for the strain of melodrama filled with dungeons, crypts, secret passageways, and other such opportunities for exploiting extreme voice effects. In a two-month season in 1938, the Mercury lineup included *Dracula, Treasure Island, A Tale of Two Cities,* and *The Count of Monte Cristo.* He took a special delight in the role of Jean Valjean in *Les Misérables* and in particular the section of the story in which Valjean comes upon the wounded Marius and carries him into the Paris sewers. *Citizen Kane* provided an abundance of such opportunities, especially with two settings — the Thatcher Library, all clanking metal and high ceilings and empty space, and the Great Hall at Xanadu, a vast echoing cavern. If some of the other flashy sound effects in the film seem to have a radio quality, this is not by accident. Welles bypassed the usual procedure of drawing effects from RKO's stock library or of having the RKO sound engineers create them and brought in his own sound specialist from radio to do some of the more unusual effects.[8] These were duly recorded and kept separately in the sound library.[9] They are now lost, but they surely would have included such things as the typewriter heard in the extreme close-up when Kane is finishing the opera review and the musical accompaniment to the light bulb that dims to signal the faltering of Susan's singing career.

Other examples of the radio influence are more subtle. Overlapping dialogue was a regular feature of the Mercury radio shows, as were other narrative devices used in the film — the use of sounds as aural punctuation, for instance, as when the closing of a door cues the end of a scene, or scene transitions in mid sentence (a device known in radio as the *cross fade*), as when Leland, talking to a crowd in the street, begins a thought, and Kane, addressing a rally in Madison Square Garden, completes it. The montage at the breakfast table may owe something of its original inspiration to this device; in some ways, it is a sophisticated visual equivalent of it. There are also similarities in the overall narrative design. The radio shows had a characteristic form: After a highly distinctive musical introduction by Bernard Herrmann, Welles himself as first-person narrator would set the scene. The action proper was a succession of emotionally high-pitched scenes involving a small number of characters, usually only two or three — in effect, sixty minutes of high spots from the literary source. They were joined by transitional narration or, more strikingly, by musical bridges; changes in the musical line cued changes of scene. *Citizen Kane* has the same heavily orchestrated musical introductions by Bernard Herrmann, a series of first-person narrators introducing their stories, an episodic structure, a tendency toward climactic scenes with sententious dialogue ("If I hadn't been rich, I might have been a really great man" or "Only you want love on your own terms"), and constant use of musical bridges to underscore scene changes. Most important of all, the radio influence is evident in the way the film uses the physical properties of sound as an element of narration.

Like other narrative forms, radio drama involves the rhetorical iteration of details on the premise that they are part of a self-contained fictional world. A fundamental difference that sets radio drama apart is that the fictive illusion depends not only on what the words say or how they are spoken but also very largely on the physical properties of the sound. Regardless of where the script tells us we are — in a drawing room, say, or by the seashore, or in a cave — our ears will only hear the dull and flat sound of a broadcasting studio unless the sound receives the appropriate acoustic manipulations. By the same token, the spatial configurations described — the locations of characters and sounds and the distances between them — must also be heard in the sounds themselves. A basic aesthetic criterion for radio drama is, How convincing are its illusions of sound location and distance? By this standard, the Mercury radio shows were among the most accomplished on the air. In *Citizen Kane*, Welles aimed for the kind of extreme sound realism that characterized the radio shows. There are good examples in the Colorado sequence, where the adult conversation in the foreground dominates the soundtrack but the tiny, distant voice of the boy playing in the snow can still be distinctly heard; in the sequence in which Kane signs the newspapers over to Thatcher, with the distance sense correctly following Kane as he moves back and forth from foreground to background; and in the Xanadu sequences, when Kane and Susan address each other from opposite ends of the Great Hall. The film has a distinct sound narrational style, in the way that it has a distinct cinematographic style. Susan's debut (the first time, from out front) provides a good illustration of how this sound style operates. The scene is very visual in its conception — an upward-moving camera carries the narrative line, and the dramatic payoff comes in a sight gag worthy of silent comedy. At the same time, the sound track carries parallel information. As the camera moves away from Susan, her voice seems to recede into the distance. This effect is achieved not by lowering the volume but by a technique from radio called fading the microphone — increasing the reverberations in a way that makes the ear hear a sound as moving away. If we close our eyes while the scene is running, the sound track alone tells us what is happening. (Welles told me, in fact, that he often applies the same test when he is directing — he turns his back and closes his eyes and listens to hear if the sounds are dramatically convincing on their own.) Throughout the film, the sound is constantly used in this way to underscore and reinforce the meaning of what we see. This is one of the reasons why *Citizen Kane* has so powerful an impact purely as story.

In the making of feature films, there are two separate and distinct sound operations, each presided over by a different sound engineer. One engineer is in charge of the sound recorded during production. In the typical studio setup, he is stationed at a console near the set, from which he is in constant communication by telephone with his production crew outside. His chief assistant is the operator of the boom — a microphone slung from a long metal rod and suspended above the actors' heads just out of camera range. This engineer's job is to adjust the level of the incoming sound, to clear up any difficulties in the pickup by contact with his boom operator, and to combine the outputs where more than one sound source is involved. In industry parlance, he is known as the production mixer.

In the early years of sound, almost all sound was produced in this way — that is, the track recorded on the set was the track used on the film. Any problems that came up had to be solved by means of retakes, and sound effects were produced and recorded right on the set. But as recording equipment became more sophisticated, so did the ability to manipulate and modify sound. In the middle to late thirties, a new studio practice rose to prominence — the rerecording of sound for improvement or enhancement during postproduction. In the sound rerecording process, certain kinds of changes in the original production sound track can be made electronically. Some portions of dialogue are recorded over again with the actors speaking in synchronization to images running silent. Tracks are recorded for material originally shot silent — montages or parts with voice-over narration, for instance. Sound effects are added. Finally, the various tracks (sometimes a dozen or more) are mixed and blended in a dubbing console into a single composite master ready for printing onto the film.

The production mixer on *Citizen Kane* was RKO veteran Bailey Fesler. Like that of many other sound engineers, Fesler's background was in radio. (He had been an engineer for an Indianapolis station.) *Citizen Kane* has to have been one of the most challenging and difficult assignments of his career because of the elaborate camera movements, the extremely complicated blocking of characters, the great variation of sound sources within some scenes, and Welles's constant demands. James G. Stewart, head of RKO's postproduction sound operation, was the rerecording engineer (sometimes called the dubbing mixer) on *Citizen Kane*. Before joining the RKO sound department in 1931, Stewart had worked in radio and as a specialist in the installation of sound equipment in motion picture theaters. (He worked on some of

James G. Stewart (left) and the master dubbing console he built for RKO in 1937. With him is another RKO sound engineer, Terry Kellum.

the major theaters on the East Coast, including Radio City Music Hall.) By 1937, he had been put in charge of all postproduction sound operations at RKO, a position he held until 1945. In 1937, he designed RKO's first master dubbing console, which was one of the most sophisticated sound-recording operations for its time (see illustration). Unlike some department heads who were only nominally involved in productions for which they received screen credit, Stewart worked on virtually every RKO film released during this period, and the high quality of sound for which RKO product was generally known can be attributed to him. Films on which he worked received nine Academy Award nominations for sound (including *Citizen Kane*), and he won three — for Best Achievement in Sound Recording on *This Land is Mine* (1943) and *The Bells of St. Mary's* (1945) and (when he was head of all technical operations for Selznick) for Best Achievement in Special Sound Effects on *Portrait of Jennie* (1948).

Since *The Magnificent Ambersons,* Welles has been known for the extensive use of looping in his films — that is, for the dubbing of speaking parts in postproduction. In *Citizen Kane,* most of the sound track is derived from the production track. Special touches were added in the rerecording process, but in many of the sequences the sound is essentially as it was recorded on the set. This gives their sound an immediacy and a spontaneity similar to the sound of the radio shows,

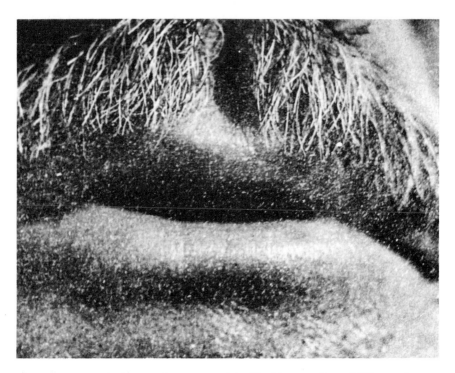

Perhaps the single most famous sound in film history — Orson Welles as the dying Kane saying the word "Rosebud". This extremely resonant whispering sound was created in the rerecording console by combining two separate tracks of Welles's voice with different reverberation times.

which were aired live. It also testifies to Welles's readiness to adapt his radio experience to the requirements of a new medium. A particularly impressive example of production sound is the musical number in the party for the *Inquirer* staff. This sequence involves the use of a multitude of sound sources of diverse quality, levels, and placement — solo lyrics, a chorus line joining in for the refrain, a marching band, a blast of trumpets, a crowd background, and the individual voices of Kane, Bernstein, and Leland. In the conversation between Bernstein and Leland, when they are seen in close shot, their dialogue is naturally loudest on the sound track, but at the same time all the other sounds — Kane's shouts in the background, the chorus refrain, the crowd noise — are all heard simultaneously, distinctly, and at the proper sound level in relation to the camera's placement. This sequence is every bit as impressive a piece of sound work as it is for its mise-en-scène and cinematography. Incidentally, as an indication of how these elements work together, such complicated effects in production sound would not have been possible without the muslin ceilings that concealed the overhead microphones.

With the dubbing console, it was as with the optical printer: Welles was quick to sense an opportunity and determined to exploit it to the limit. The rerecording process, like the film's special effects, took much longer than expected and went far over budget — $16,996 in actual costs, as against an original estimate of $7,288. Besides the enhanced quality and range of individual effects, sound re-recording opened up broader possibilities. For actions that would have been difficult or impossible to shoot with production sound, sound could be added later. The final sequence in the Great Hall provides an example. A tremendous sense of space is absolutely essential to the dramatic concept of this scene. Overhead microphones would have seriously inhibited the camera's movements and range. The entire sequence was shot silent, much of it in long shot, and the actors recorded their dialogue in postproduction.

Sound rerecording also makes it possible to build up a very complex set of effects. The most technically sophisticated sound sequence created in postproduction is the Madison Square Garden rally. The sound problem here was the same as the special effects problem — how to create the sense and feeling of such an event artificially. In the track that was recorded, Welles delivered the campaign speech. In radio, Welles had learned how to manipulate his voice to suit the locale called for in the script. (In real life, we do this naturally without being aware of it: We tend to speak faster in an enclosed space without many sound-reflecting surfaces and slower in a larger, more reverberant space.) He spoke as he would have in the actual situation — more slowly and pausing slightly at the ends of phrases and sentences. In the recording console, the reverberation rate of his voice was manipulated to produce the echo chamber effect. As an added touch of realism, about a dozen variant copies of the original recording were made, each with a different sound quality, and bits and pieces from one or another of these were dubbed into the pauses. If we listen closely, we can hear actual snippets of dialogue sounding like echoes between sentences and phrases. And even the echo effects are very carefully calibrated: shorter and less pronounced when the camera is close to the speaker, delayed and more reverberant in the reaction shots of the audience.

Stewart credits Welles with the sound concepts in this sequence and says that most of the ideas involving the use of sound in the film came from Welles. Working with Welles, he adds, was one of the most significant experiences of his own professional career: Much of what he knows aesthetically about sound he says he learned from him.

MUSIC

Composer Bernard Herrmann had been doing scores for the Mercury Theatre radio shows since 1936. Welles first brought him to Hollywood to write the music for *Heart of Darkness*. His contract was for twelve weeks and a $10,000 fee. He was brought back for *Citizen Kane* under similar terms. Herrmann himself explains the significance of his contract:

> I had heard of the many handicaps that exist for a composer in Hollywood. One was the great speed with which scores often had to be written — sometimes in as little as two or three weeks. . . . I was given . . . ample time to think about the film and to work out a general artistic plan for the score . . . [and] to do my own orchestration and conducting.
>
> I worked on the film, reel by reel, as it was being shot and cut. In this way I had a sense of the picture being built, and of my own music being a part of that building.[10]

The classical Hollywood approach to film scoring is represented in the works of such composers as Max Steiner, Erich Wolfgang Korngold, and Miklos Rosza. Its idiom is late nineteenth-century European romanticism, particularly Wagner, Mahler, and Richard Strauss. The main features are full symphonic scoring, lush orchestration, the use of melodies as leitmotifs, and the underscoring of the dramatic action by the music. Herrmann's approach was very different. Instead of scoring for a full orchestra, he used smaller groupings of instruments and freely employed unorthodox combinations. For the opening sequence of *Citizen Kane,* for instance, he used three bass flutes, two clarinets, three bass clarinets, three bassoons, a contrabassoon, four French horns, three trumpets, three trombones, a vibraphone, kettledrums, gong, bass drum, and bass viols.[11] Only the opera sequences and the ending are scored for a full symphony orchestra. Herrmann uses leitmotifs — as we shall see, the entire score of *Citizen Kane* is structured around them — but his basic unit is a brief phrase of a few notes, not an extended melody. Hollywood scoring is most often associated with overstated orchestrations (especially strings) in scenes of gusty emotion. In typical Hollywood practice, the sequence of Kane's boyhood in Colorado would be ripe for such treatment. In contrast, the little musical accompaniment that Herrmann provides is very subdued and restrained — muted horns, a single clarinet, an oboe, light strings, soft bassoons. Generally, when he uses underscoring in dialogue scenes, it is very understated. (An exception comes after Susan's suicide attempt, when the music of her aria is heard in a dissonant key.) The avoidance of underscoring is probably a sign of Herrmann's long experience in radio, where music played as background to dialogue was distractive. Herrmann himself was very aware of the influence of radio on his work, particularly in the use of musical cues to announce scene transitions. Another radio practice is the use of lively, upbeat musical interludes to indicate the passage of time. Equivalents in the film are the series of spirited musical forms accompanying the running-a-newspaper montages — a galop with "Traction Trust Exposed," a cancan scherzo with the circulation buildup, and so on. Herrmann came up with the idea for these from reading the script and, in

The studio score used for recording.

another departure from Hollywood tradition, convinced Welles to let him write the music first and edit the images to it.

Herrmann went on the RKO payroll October 21 and worked for fourteen weeks. The last two weeks were spent supervising the rerecording process to ensure that his intentions in regard to sound level and dynamics were faithfully realized. The main concept in his score can be traced to an idea of Welles's. The script originally called only for a band and dancing girls in the publisher's party sequence. Welles decided to add the vocal number extolling the virtues of Kane. He selected a Mexican song, "A Poco No," by Pepe Guizar, for the music, and commissioned songwriter Herman Ruby to write new lyrics. In the request for permission, the Music Department indicated that Welles wanted wholesale clearance and "might use it as the theme of the picture."[12] That is precisely what Herrmann did in the music. He used the first four notes of the song, which accompany the words *There is a man,* as the basis for one of the film's two main leitmotifs. He called this motif "Power." It is first heard in the opening two bars of the score in muted brass. The second is the "Rosebud" theme, intermingled first with the "Power" theme, then heard distinctly and separately as a vibraphone solo when we see the glass globe. Musically, the two motifs are complementary. Like the painting of Xanadu, they embody the contradiction of Kane — the clash between the romantic ideal of childhood innocence and the corrupting influences of adulthood. They are repeated, whole or in part, in a multitude of variations throughout the score. The variations follow the story line. Melodically and orchestrally purer in the earlier parts of Kane's life, they become increasingly dark and dissonant as the film progresses. When the burning sled is revealed, they are played as a single continuous melody by a full orchestra.[13]

Musical motifs are also used for other characters. On Thompson's visit to Thatcher Library, muted, flatulent horns parody the Dies Irae at the sight of the statue, and this theme is later repeated. Emily is associated with the waltz form, as when she is first seen outside the *Inquirer* building. The breakfast table montage is accompanied by a waltz theme that undergoes a series of increasingly discordant variations as the marriage deteriorates. If Emily has the graceful elegance of Waldteufel, the sound track associates Susan with the brash, lowlife sensuality of jazz. When Thompson visits the nightclub, the background theme is taken from "In a Mizz," a 1930s jazz number by Charles Barrett and Haven Johnson. This is the song performed at the picnic in the Everglades.

The main operatic conceptions in the film originated with Welles. (Welles told me he has been an opera buff all his life.) The *"Una voce poco fa"* aria from *The Barber of Seville* is sung in a small, untrained voice with faulty breath support, bad diction, and bad pitch. When Susan is unable to hit the note for Signor Matisti as Kane looks on, the voice is a half-step flat. In the script, Massenet's *Thaïs* is specified as the opera for Susan's debut; this is said to be an elaborate in-joke by Mankiewicz involving Hearst and a one-time fiancée who was an opera singer. Welles considered using the mirror scene from *Thaïs* at first, but RKO failed to secure clearance. Anyway, there was a dramatic problem — *Thaïs* does not open with a soprano in midaria (no other opera does either, for that matter). So he decided to ask Herrmann to compose an original piece with some unusual specifications. These are outlined in a wire of July 18.[14] The opera should be French Oriental in nature, with a big, flamboyant historical production number. Welles thinks of it as a parody of the typical Mary Garden vehicles he had seen in his youth. (Garden was the colorful prima donna of the Chicago Opera who specialized in such roles as Salome, Thaïs, and Mélisande.) He suggests Ernest Reyer's *Salammbô,* which, he says, would provide the opportunity for Susan to dress like a "grand opera neoclassical courtesan." He points out the logical improbability in the script that Susan is singing the same aria when the curtain goes up as when it goes down, but he says if this is handled deftly no one will notice. From these guidelines, Herrmann came up with the similarly titled *Salaambo,* richly orchestrated in the manner of Richard Strauss, with a libretto borrowed from Racine's *Phèdre.* His own special touch was to write the part for a voice far exceeding the singer's capabilities — "in a very high tessitura, so that a girl with a modest voice would be completely hopeless in it."[15] A young soprano from the San Francisco opera, Jean Forward, was commissioned to dub Susan's role in *Salaambo.* She is not singing badly, as is often stated; she simply is singing in a key too high for her voice. That, combined with the overpowering orchestration, gave the effect that Herrmann desired — that she was struggling hopelessly "in quicksand."[16]

Herrmann's score for *Citizen Kane* was nominated for an Academy Award, but it lost to another Herrmannn score, for *The Devil and Daniel Webster (All That Money Can Buy).* Herrmann also did *The Magnificent Ambersons* but insisted that his name be removed after the music was tampered with when the studio recut that film. Although he never worked with Welles again, he continued to work in films. With his film music, as on *The Magnificent Ambersons,* he always insisted on having the final say. The reason, according to him, is that most film directors, Hitchcock included, have terrible musical taste. Welles, he says, is an exception: Him he characterizes as "a man of great musical culture."[17]

EDITING

The film's editor was Robert Wise. He replaced an older editor originally assigned to the film who did not suit Welles. Wise had limited experience but was probably considered a good choice because he was closer to Welles's age and had been helpful to another young director, Garson Kanin, on some of his early films. The editor is the technical coordinator of the postproduction phase. He monitors the work of the various departments to see that photographic and aural values are uniform and consistent. Once these things are assured, he selects the shots that are to be used, assembles them in the proper story continuity, makes the necessary adjustments in the relation of shots to one another, and fixes the length of each individual shot. The amount of creative influence he exerts in this process depends on the amount of freedom the producer or director allows him and on the state the footage is in at the time when he receives it.

Wise says that Welles would give him instructions and leave him alone to do his work. Welles seems to have been generally pleased with the results — as he was not with the special effects and the sound, where he rejected a lot and insisted that it be done over again. This is partly a tribute to Wise's skills, but we must also recognize something more fundamental in the nature of the film. Wise says that, from the very first footage, it was obvious that *Citizen Kane* was a "very carefully thought out and planned picture."[18] Another way of saying this is that the film was largely preedited: The footage itself tended to dictate the way it would be cut. Welles says that one of the first things he learned from Toland was how to edit in the camera. Most of *Citizen Kane* was shot with only one camera, without any covering footage and, Welles says on Toland's advice, with practically no close-ups or reaction shots. This made it virtually impossible to tamper with the unusually long takes that are the hallmark of the film's cinematographic style. The use of overlapping dialogue also greatly inhibits cutting in these scenes. We know from Herrmann that some of the montage sequences were scored first, then edited to fit the music. As we have seen, many of the film's unusual and justly famous narrative transitions were made by Toland in the camera or by Dunn with the optical printer. "News on the March," a tour de force of editing of its type, was done by the RKO newsreel department, because Welles felt they could best capture the spirit of the original.[19]

The most celebrated piece of editing in the film is the breakfast table montage. Wise says it took him weeks to get it right. The interworking of dialogue and image is especially subtle, as in this sequence:

(on swish pan)	*Emily:* Charles . . .
(on Emily)	do you know how long you kept me waiting last night while you . . .
(on Kane)	went to the newspaper for ten minutes?
(on Emily)	What do you do on a newspaper in the middle of the night? *Kane:* Emily . . .
(on Kane)	my dear, your only corespondent is the *Inquirer.*

At the same time, the basic concept had been in the script, the shots were planned in terms of it, and Herrmann recorded the waltz medley in advance of the editing; Wise's contribution, as in the example cited here, mainly involved the rhythm and pace. When I asked Wise for another example of good editing in the film, he mentioned the love nest encounter. But in that sequence, too, he worked within a carefully prescribed framework. Of the fourteen shots (beginning and ending on the stairway), six are extended continuous takes. Almost 70 percent of the total running time is in the first four shots, which are respectively twenty-eight, twenty-four, one hundred seventeen, and twenty-four seconds. Two other lengthy shots, nine and ten (twenty and forty-six seconds respectively), account for another 23 percent of the total. There is intercutting at only two points, in sequences totaling less than twenty seconds of screen time in all. In one of these, the camera setups dictate a somewhat unconventional use of space — a high overhead view down the stairwell (shot eleven) following a shot from inside the apartment, and a close shot of Kane ranting on the landing (shot thirteen) between two long shots from the bottom of the stairway. Few films can have left an editor with a narrower range of choices.

RELEASE

By running a closed set, limiting access to rushes, and carefully managing the publicity, Welles had kept the Hearst connection relatively quiet. For instance, a feature article on the film in the December 1940 issue of *Stage* summarizes the story and compares it with the "Faust legend" without ever mentioning Hearst.[20] Inevitably, the storm broke. RKO hoped to open the film in mid February. Writers for national magazines had early deadlines, so a rough cut was previewed for a select few on January 3. When an advance leak in *Hollywood Reporter* described this as a showing for a "group of friends,"[21] Welles was forced to apologize to Hedda Hopper and invite her also because of a long-standing promise that she would be the first to see the film.[22] Meanwhile, *Friday* magazine had an article set to run in its next issue that drew point-by-point comparisons between Kane and Hearst. According to *Hollywood Reporter,* the code of silence had been broken by Mercury players returning East.[23] The *Friday* article mentions the advance buildup that Louella Parsons, Hollywood correspondent for Hearst papers, had been giving the film and quotes Welles as saying, "Wait until the woman finds out that the picture's about her boss."[24] When Parsons got wind of this, she was furious: Her archrival had gotten the scoop, Welles had led her on, and she had been made a fool of in public. She demanded, and got, an immediate preview of her own, which she attended in company with attorneys for Hearst. James Stewart, who was present, says she stalked out while the film was still running.[25] Shortly after, an RKO secretary took an urgent phone call from Parsons to Schaefer threatening RKO with "one of 'the most beautiful lawsuits' in history if they release *Citizen Kane.*"[26] Next day, the front-page headline in *Daily Variety* read, "HEARST BANS RKO FROM PAPERS." The accompanying story indicated that the edict had already been put into effect and that a review of *Kitty Foyle* had been yanked from late editions of the previous day's *Los Angeles Examiner.*[27]

The ban was short-lived: After two weeks it was lifted for everything but mention of *Citizen Kane* itself. Apparently the possibility of legal action was only briefly considered. The legal grounds were hazy, and a court case would inevitably draw attention to the film and make people sympathetic toward it. Instead, Hearst's people (if not with Hearst's outright backing, then certainly at least with his tacit assent)[28] decided to concentrate on the weakest link: the almost paranoid fear in the film industry of being held up to public exposure. A warning was issued almost at once. On January 13, a front-page story in *Hollywood Reporter* carried a claim, attributed to "authoritative Hearst sources," that Hearst papers were about to begin a series of editorials attacking Hollywood's practice of hiring refugees and immigrants for jobs that could be held by Americans. The deliberate aim, the article went on, was to bring pressure on the other studios to force RKO to shelve *Citizen Kane.* Meanwhile, Louella Parsons began waging a one-person campaign of intimidation by telephone. The strategy worked: In a short time, George Schaefer was approached by Nicholas Schenck, head of MGM's parent company,

Virtually all discussion of the use of Hearst in the film has been on the level of story. However, Hearst was also a frequent visual source. The shot at right of Kane delivering a campaign speech is modeled on the cover illustration (above) from the *Saturday Review of Literature* of April 25, 1936.

with an offer on behalf of Louis B. Mayer and other Hollywood executives to reimburse RKO its total picture cost if it would destroy the film.[29]

Schaefer's lawyers had originally cleared the script.[30] When the trouble with Hearst broke out, RKO's New York legal team, along with one of Hollywood's leading attorneys, Mendel Silberberg, screened the film, and reassured Schaefer once again. On January 21, RKO gave its official reply — the film would be released as scheduled with one of the largest promotional campaigns in the studio's history. In the months to come, Schaefer would be buffeted from all sides, and he would be forced to postpone the opening more than once, but he did not waver from his original determination.

Schaefer handled the buyout offer by bringing Welles in from California for a private screening of the film with the New York corporate heads of the studios and their lawyers. Robert Wise, who went along to handle technical details, was present at this screening and says that afterwards Welles made an absolutely brilliant and compelling presentation on why the film had to be released. Shortly after, word was passed that there would be no objection to the release provided that certain changes were made. Wise says that these were all minor and involved

softening up specific references that might be offensive to Hearst and that Welles assented to them.[31] Wise did the reediting in New York and telephoned the changes to his assistant Mark Robson in Hollywood. Apparently no record of these changes has survived, but by comparing the shooting script with the cutting continuity we can infer with reasonable certainty what they consisted of — several references to Hearst by name in the newsreel; inflammatory associations, such as the McKinley assassination; references to specific political issues, such as Hearst's stand on income tax; several allusions to Susan's drinking problem; some extremely negative characterizations of Kane in Thatcher's manuscript; Leland's reference to Kane as a bad newspaperman; some topical allusions in the political campaign; and an extremely blunt passage in Thompson's final summation. Schaefer told Kael that as an added precaution he consulted Time, Inc.'s specialist on invasion of privacy and was advised to make one final change:[32] As originally filmed, Raymond said to Thompson, "He was a little gone in the head" and re-peated this statement later in the conversation; actor Paul Stewart dubbed in sub-stitute lines: "He acted" (and, later, "the old man acted") "kind of funny some-times."[33] The print Wise took to New York on January 27 had a running time of two hours, two minutes, and forty seconds. The final corrected version shipped from Hollywood on February 13 ran one hour, fifty-nine minutes, and sixteen seconds.[34] This time it was run with just the lawyers from the various corporations in attendance,[35] and they pronounced themselves satisfied.

Other publishers besides Hearst were used for visual lore. The photograph that comes to life in *Citizen Kane* is modeled after the photograph above of James Gordon Bennett's staff on the *New York Herald*. Below, the *Inquirer* staff from the film.

Although the major issue had been settled, the trouble was far from over. The campaign of harassment against RKO resumed. Schaefer was pilloried on the front page of Hearst papers from coast to coast on an unrelated matter, a minor lawsuit brought by an author against RKO for breach of contract. In the *New York Mirror* of Sunday February 16, the case was cited as text for a column by the paper's film critic on how Hollywood corporations take advantage of the unsuspecting and innocent. Welles was also made to feel the pressure. There were reports of mysterious journalistic inquiries to his draft board. Hearst papers played up an attack by the American Legion on a Welles radio show, "His Honor, the Mayor" ("The Free Company," CBS, April 6), as un-American and subversive; not coincidentally, a Hearst reporter was publicity chief for the Legion. Radio City Music Hall decided not to open *Citizen Kane* after all; Schaefer told Kael it was because of an implied threat by Louella Parsons to Nelson Rockefeller that a defamatory story on his grandfather in Hearst's *American Weekly* might be a possible consequence. For fear of retaliation, other exhibitors also refused to handle the film, so that Schaefer and his sales organization were forced to line up what theaters they could on their own. Welles was growing increasingly impatient, and when these complications caused additional delays, he threatened RKO with a lawsuit. When the release arrangements were finally worked out, Hearst papers refused to accept advertising for the film.[36]

Schaefer pressed ahead on all fronts. As a conciliatory gesture, he arranged early in February for a print of the film to be shipped to San Simeon. Apparently Hearst never looked at it: James Stewart, who was working with Mark Robson, says that, when it came back, the special seals they had placed on individual reels were unbroken.[37] Schaefer softened up the opposition in Hollywood by making sure that the film was widely seen. There were special previews in RKO's screening rooms throughout February and March, sometimes more than one the same evening. The guest lists were studded with Hollywood royalty. The one for March 6, for instance, included Cary Grant, David O. Selznick, Roy Disney, Walter Wanger, Jesse Lasky, Samuel Goldwyn, Leo McCarey, Harry Cohn, and William Wyler.[38] Predictably, there was considerable internal dissension within RKO's New York office. Schaefer seems to have gotten around it by bypassing his board of directors on key issues. He told Kael he did not take the buyout offer to them because he suspected they would advise him to accept it. Announcement of the final release plan for the film was made in advance of a board meeting at which the matter was to be considered. The opening engagements would be in New York, Chicago, and Los Angeles; all three cities had powerful Hearst newspapers.[39]

Citizen Kane opened at the RKO Palace on Broadway in New York on May 1. It opened in Chicago on May 6 and in Los Angeles on May 8. In all three cities, theaters not intended for major openings had to be used, and they were specially refurbished for the purpose. Later in the month, the film opened in Boston, San Francisco, and Washington. These were roadshow engagements at advanced prices and sometimes with reserved seating. Coincidentally, a report came out at this time that the attack on Welles's radio show had more than doubled the ratings

George Schaefer in his moment of triumph: the New York opening of *Citizen Kane*. Welles is with Dolores Del Rio, and he is being spoken to by Elsa Maxwell.

for the series.[40] Apparently the Hearst people got the point: The editorial attacks in the Hearst press ceased, though Hearst papers still continued to refuse advertising. The critical reception was overwhelmingly favorable; Kael is probably right that *Citizen Kane* was "more highly praised by the American press than any other movie in history."[41] It was frequently cited as a historical turning point:

Tonight I was present at the birth of a new art form: The Motion Picture.

One of the most interesting and technically superior films that has ever come out of a Hollywood studio.

Staggering and belongs at once among the great screen achievements.

The boldest free-hand stroke in major screen production since Griffith and Bitzer were running wild to unshackle the camera.

One of the outstanding films of all time.[42]

But there was trouble at the box office from the beginning. The roadshow campaign was a disappointment. In the wider run at regular prices during the fall, the results were much better in cities and larger towns, but in remoter locations business continued to be average to poor. RKO also continued to have trouble getting exhibitors to play the film. One chain controlling more than 500 theaters got *Citizen Kane* as part of a package but refused to play it, reportedly out of fear of Hearst. In these locations, arrangements with independent exhibitors had to be made if the film played at all.[43] Undoubtedly the distribution problems hurt, but it is unlikely that they made a crucial difference; *Citizen Kane* is simply not a film for an ordinary commercial audience. Late in the year, both the New York Film Critics and the National Board of Review voted *Citizen Kane* best picture of 1941. There were also Academy Award nominations in nine major categories — best picture, actor, director, screenplay, cinematography, art direction, sound recording, editing, and music score. It was widely thought that a sweep was in the offing, and this would, of course, have made for new life at the box office. But the film won in only one category, best original screenplay, and the award was shared by Mankiewicz and Welles. A strong element of vindictiveness seems to have been involved: According to *Variety,* block voting against Welles by screen extras deprived him of the best picture and actor awards, and there were probably similar prejudices at work in the special panel of insiders who decided the technical awards.[44]

After the ordeal with Hearst, the exhibition nightmares, and the disappointments of Oscar night, it was probably with some relief that RKO retired *Citizen Kane* to the vaults after its play-off in 1942. At the time, it was carried on company books at a loss of more than $150,000. Through the rest of the decade, it played a few brief engagements at big-city retrospective houses. (On one such occasion, a patron complained to the *New York Times* that the version he saw lacked the opening scenes at Xanadu and Kane's death.)[45] But after 1950, it virtually disappeared. For instance, there is not a single listing of *Citizen Kane* in *The New Yorker*'s theater schedules between January 24, 1950 and February 20, 1956. During this absence, the film's reputation among English-language critics began to slip. Richard Griffith, updating Paul Rotha's landmark *The Film Till Now* in 1949, dismissed *Citizen Kane* as "tinpot if not crackpot Freud" and as essentially a flashy but vacuous display of cinematic techniques.[46] In his milestone survey *The Liveliest Art* (1957), Arthur Knight passed over *Citizen Kane* in favor of *The Magnificent Ambersons* and wrote off Welles, as a film director, as "no longer a major force."[47]

Elsewhere, however, the film's critical reputation was flourishing. American films were shut out of France during the German occupation; *Citizen Kane* did not play in Paris until 1946. Surprisingly, it was disparaged by a number of well-known people, including Jean-Paul Sartre and film historian Georges Sadoul. However, the press reviews were generally enthusiastic. Most important for the long run was the attention given to the film in the little magazines.[48] In its December 1946 issue, *La Revue du cinéma,* the forerunner of *Cahiers du cinéma,* printed a script extract from *Citizen Kane,* the production history of the film from Fowler's biography, and a critical essay that dealt with the film's Proustian elements, plus a script extract and a long review of *The Magnificent Ambersons.* Subsequent issues were filled with *Citizen Kane* and other Welles material, including a translation of one of Gregg Toland's articles and André Bazin's two-part study of William Wyler's mise-en-scène camera style.[49] Bazin was, of course, the one who did the most to enhance the film's reputation. In Welles and Toland's long takes and composition in depth, Bazin found an aesthetic of reality that was fundamentally different from the older montage tradition that descended from Griffith and the Soviets. He elaborated on the implications of this difference in *Orson Welles* (1950), which contains the famous extended analysis of the shot with Susan and the medicine bottle after her suicide attempt.[50] In "The Evolution of the Language of Cinema," his most influential essay, Bazin characterized *Citizen Kane* as a fountainhead in the development of film as an art form:

If we have dwelt at some length on Orson Welles it is because the date of his appearance in the filmic firmament (1941) marks more or less the beginning of a new period and also because his case is the most spectacular and, by virtue of his very excesses, the most significant.[51]

Bazin's younger colleagues on *Cahiers du cinéma* were equally rhapsodic, though their praise sprang from much more personal motives. Truffaut: "To shoot *Citizen Kane* at twenty-five years of age, is this not the dream of all the young habitués of the cinémathèques?"[52] Godard: "When Orson Welles made *Citizen Kane* he was twenty-five years old. Since then, young film-makers the world over have dreamed of nothing but making their first big film before reaching that age."[53]

The vicissitudes of the film's critical fortunes are illustrated in statistical surveys. In 1952, the British film magazine *Sight and Sound* asked a panel of leading critics to select the all-time best films. *The Bicycle Thieves* came in first, a sign of the ascendancy of social realism in the postwar era. *Citizen Kane* did not make the top ten (twelve, actually, because of ties), but it was listed as a runner-up. Only ten years later, however, in *Sight and Sound*'s second poll, *Citizen Kane* was first. The general explanation for what happened in the intervening decade is the sudden and dramatic rise of serious interest in the Hollywood studio film, which took place in

the middle 1950s. Several developments occurring simultaneously had contributed to this phenomenon. One was the licensing of the studio libraries for showing
on television. Suddenly, in the late 1950s, hundreds of old Hollywood films, many
not seen for decades, were available on virtually a round-the-clock basis. Another
was the emergence of the art house and film society circuits. These served the
functions that the cinémathèques and ciné clubs had served in France: They provided mechanisms for reasoned film programming and forums for intellectual
debate. They also stimulated the production of written criticism. For instance,
New York Film Bulletin, one important conduit through which French film criticism was introduced to the United States, began as a program calendar; Pauline
Kael got her start as a film critic writing program notes for a Berkeley retrospective house; Joseph McBride's *Orson Welles* (like many other books and articles)
grew out of film society activities. Finally, the auteur movement in criticism
helped to give the interest in the history of Hollywood an intellectual rationale and
thematic core. "Like the movies of Renoir, Chaplin or John Ford, the films of
Orson Welles are distinctively autographed by their maker." The opening statement in Peter Bogdanovich's program monograph accompanying the 1961 Museum of Modern Art Welles retrospective (a landmark event in the rehabilitation
of his reputation) provides the key to why *Citizen Kane* has occupied such a privileged position with auteur critics on both sides of the Atlantic.[54] Of all major
Hollywood films, *Citizen Kane* is the one that most boldly and emphatically announces an artistic personality.

Coincidentally, RKO's was the first of the major studio libraries to be sold to
television.[55] *Citizen Kane* began appearing on the small screen early in 1956. At
about the same time, the film was rereleased theatrically to cash in on the publicity surrounding Welles's return to Broadway in *King Lear.* Andrew Sarris wrote a
classic essay on the film in connection with this revival. (It appeared in *Film Culture,* no. 9, 1956. This magazine is as important in its own right as *Cahiers du
cinéma.* Though it is mainly associated now with independent filmmakers, in its
early days it was the major outlet for the American auteur movement. In the mid
1950s, before the influence of the French began to be felt, Sarris and Eugene
Archer, the cofounder of the movement, were both publishing auteur criticism in
Film Culture.[56] Sarris's legendary ranking of American directors first appeared as
a special feature in this magazine.) The essay *"Citizen Kane:* The American Baroque" is of special importance for its attempt to take the film out of historical and
biographical contexts (the connection with Hearst, the Welles legend, and so on)
and to deal with its thematic implications head-on; in this way, it anticipates much
of what has been written since.[57]

The underlying motive of Sarris's essay was to vindicate the received proposition
that *Citizen Kane* is "the great American film." In his auteur catalogue of directors
published a few years later, Welles was in the pantheon, and *Citizen Kane* was "the
work that influenced the cinema more profoundly than any American film since
Birth of a Nation."[58] As the film remained in continuous circulation in one format or
another after the rerelease, these precepts began to gain widespread acceptance.

During the 1960s, *Citizen Kane* became the single most written about film. A key publication was Peter Cowie's *The Cinema of Orson Welles,* the first critical monograph in English and a formal prototype of such later studies as Higham's, McBride's, and Naremore's — auteurist in approach, with a hefty lead chapter on *Citizen Kane* ("The Study of a Colossus"), and the later films measured according to how they lived up to its achievement.[59] Ronald Gottesman's *Focus on "Citizen Kane,"* a collection of important reviews, background pieces, and critical statements, was designed for the rapidly expanding academic market. Pauline Kael occupies a special place in the evolution of the film's reputation. Her target was Welles, not the film; "Raising Kane" wholeheartedly endorsed the proposition that *Citizen Kane* was the great American film and in fact served to promote the message to a much wider audience than it had reached before.

Citizen Kane was in an even more solid first place in the third *Sight and Sound* poll in 1972. During that bicentennial-conscious decade, several organizations conducted similar canvasses to determine the "great American films." The Los Angeles International Film Exposition (Filmex) polled forty prominent American film reviewers, critics, and historians. The University of Southern California Performing Arts Council added industry representation to its convocation of respondents. *American Film* enfranchised its entire readership — a mix of industry people, cognoscenti, and the general public. In reporting the *American Film* story, National Public Radio (NPR) conducted its own poll of listeners. *Citizen Kane* was first in the Filmex and NPR polls, it tied for first with *Gone With the Wind* in USC's poll, and it ran a close second to *Gone With the Wind* in the *American Film* survey, where it outranked such crowd pleasers as *Star Wars* and *2001* and such all-time popular favorites as *Casablanca, The Wizard of Oz, Singin' in the Rain,* and *The African Queen.*[60] The big surprise in these results is not the critical unanimity but the widespread industry and popular support. Clearly, by that time what had begun as the critics' pick had become the common view. At about the same time, *Citizen Kane* also succeeded in penetrating the academic world. A survey conducted in 1975 and 1976 by the American Film Institute revealed that *Citizen Kane* was used in more college and university film classes than any other film, and it was named almost twice as often as the second place runner-up, *Battleship Potemkin.*[61] In 1976, *PMLA,* the ultimate establishment journal in scholarly literary studies, published its first film article ever, an analysis of the meanings of Rosebud in *Citizen Kane.*[62] To come full circle, in the 1982 *Sight and Sound* poll, *Citizen Kane* was again first.[63] Into the 1980s, *Citizen Kane* remains critically entrenched as a towering force in the history of film and the standard by which all other films are to be judged.

6

Collaboration and
The Magnificent Ambersons

After *Citizen Kane,* Welles undertook two other projects at RKO that were both potentially of equal significance. A completely realized *Magnificent Ambersons* might have been as important a film as *Citizen Kane* is. A finished *It's All True,* a four-part anthology of stories and sketches on diverse subjects, might indeed have accomplished what Welles originally intended — the start of a revolution against standard Hollywood entertainment programming. But *The Magnificent Ambersons* went disastrously over budget, got very mixed reactions at previews, and, without Welles around to fight for it, was severely recut by the studio. *It's All True* sank into an even deeper morass of its own in South America. The histories of both these ill-fated productions are enormously complex, and each deserves a full and separate treatment on its own. For *The Magnificent Ambersons,* in the presumed absence of any surviving record on film, we need as full a reconstruction of the original version as is possible from secondary sources, such as scripts and still photographs of missing scenes. But one part of the story of *The Magnificent Ambersons* is directly pertinent to my main theme. As I shall show, problems of collaboration were a major factor in this film's ultimate undoing.

Welles originally decided on a political espionage thriller as his follow-up to *Citizen Kane.* The source novel was Alexander Calder-Marshall's *The Way to Santiago* (1940), a kind of *Smiler With the Knife* with a Mexican setting: A homegrown fascist movement is secretly trading oil to the Nazis for arms and stockpiling these for use in an insurrection against the democratic government. The conspiracy is led by the mysterious Señor Tom, who in his undercover identity is the respected Mexican correspondent for a British newspaper. After an older colleague on the trail of the story is killed, a young reporter gets involved, sniffs out the plot, braves perils of all sorts, and emerges to save the day. Welles started the screenplay while *Citizen Kane* was still in production and continued to work on it over the winter while he was in New York directing a stage version of Richard Wright's *Native Son.* His main story changes involved the principal characters. He invented a new villain based on an actual person then in the news: William Joyce, a British subject who joined the Nazis, moved to Germany at the beginning of the war, and, as the notorious Lord Haw Haw, broadcast German propaganda to England. Welles's villain has been recruited by the conspiracy to broadcast propaganda favoring the insurrection as part of an effort to ensure that the United States will remain neutral. The hero is a lookalike of the villain (this would enable Welles to play both parts) who gets caught up in the events through mistaken identity. As the story opens, the hero, who has been attacked by the villain's enemies, regains consciousness in a police station; he is suffering from amnesia, and everyone thinks him to be his lookalike. He goes along at first, because for all he knows he is that person. Gradually he learns that he is not, but he continues to play along with the plan in order to get to the bottom of things. Eventually, at Santiago, the nerve center of the conspiracy, he is found out and brought face to face with his counterpart. But at a crucial moment, he outwits the conspirators, takes over their radio transmitter, and exposes the plot over the air. Welles added a Mexican heroine, a part he intended for his current romantic attachment, actress Dolores Del Rio.[1]

As had become his custom, Welles asked for Amalia Kent to help him with the script, but she was already on assignment. On Schaefer's personal okay, Perry Ferguson was allowed to go to New York to start work with Welles.[2] Gregg Toland was dispatched to Mexico to scout locations and make other arrangements. (Apparently Welles had received some kind of tentative commitment for Toland from Samuel Goldwyn.) Mercury assistant Richard Baer shuttled between Hollywood and New York coordinating the planning. In view of the quality of the talent involved and the special pains he was taking, it appears that Welles had something considerably more ambitious than *Smiler With the Knife* in mind. He promoted the venture to Schaefer as a potential breakthrough in the treatment of Latin Americans on the screen and as a gesture of hemispheric unity that would be welcomed by Washington and the Mexicans alike.[3] But despite these assurances and an active lobbying effort by Del Rio back home, the Mexican government denied Welles permission to shoot the film in Mexico. According to *Variety,* this was motivated by Mexico's desire to preserve good diplomatic relations with Germany.[4] Welles countered that he could still shoot the picture in the United States, but that did not really get to the heart of RKO's problem with the venture. The studio feared that the subject matter would finally prove offensive to the Mexicans, and with the European market already gone because of the war, to risk the Latin American market as well would be to court financial disaster. Besides, Schaefer had officially committed the studio to a policy of keeping strictly out of the politics of the war. Consequently, Welles was unable to get RKO's approval to proceed. Nevertheless, he kept the Mexican story on his list of impending films and continued trying to sell the studio on it for some time (including once just after Pearl Harbor, when he assured them he now had clearance from the Mexican government).[5] Undoubtedly, he strongly believed in the project, but there is also a hint of wish-fulfillment in the idea of the draft-exempt Welles's playing a radio broadcaster who is influential in shaping the course of great wartime events.

With *The Way to Santiago,* Welles was moving toward the formation of a production repertory company, with himself as director and writer, Kent as his special writing assistant, and Ferguson and Toland in the other key roles. If he had succeeded, the entire story of his career might be different. As it was, the collapse of the project left him in a *Heart of Darkness* situation all over again — several months along without even a story in development. At this point, he reviewed more than forty possible subjects with an RKO story editor — everything from a life of Beethoven to *The Brothers Karamazov* and *To Have and Have Not.*[6] Schaefer continued to impress on Welles the need to do something quick and commercial to belie his profligate image and establish his financial credibility. Without question, *Citizen Kane* would enhance his artistic reputation, but it was extremely long in coming, it was a financial question mark, and there was still the matter of well over a hundred thousand dollars expended on questionable projects that would almost surely never see the light of day. Schaefer suggested *Journey into Fear,* an Eric Ambler espionage thriller already in development that had a screenplay by Ben Hecht. Welles expressed interest on condition that he could throw out everything that had already been done and start over again in his own way. He surely sensed, however, that following up *Citizen Kane* with something of that sort would amount to a tremendous comedown. He had a bold idea for a four-part story anthology, but it would require a lot of preparation. Like *Citizen Kane, The Magnificent Ambersons* came about partly out of desperation. The Mercury Theatre had done Tarkington's novel as a radio show on October 29, 1939, with Welles in the role of George Minafer, Walter Huston as Eugene Morgan, and Nan Sunderland (Mrs. Walter Huston) as Isabel. A historical regional color novel is not the kind of property one readily associates with RKO. To sell Schaefer on it, Welles went in to see him alone, played portions of the Mercury broadcast, and exercised all his charm and powers of persuasion. Once again, the two worked out a compromise. Under a new and separate contract, Welles would produce, direct, and write the screenplay for *The Magnificent Ambersons* and *Journey into Fear,* and he would also appear as an actor in the latter without additional pay. Under the new arrangement, RKO would have tighter control, such as script and casting approval. Most significantly, Welles gave up the right of final cut. These two productions would be first in order, after which Welles would still owe the two due in the original contract. The first of these would be the *It's All True* story anthology, which at this time was being planned with all North American settings and subjects.[7]

Welles himself undertook to write the *Magnificent Ambersons* screenplay. Amalia Kent was available again. Welles devised the opening montage and blocked out the rest directly from the source novel, and Kent was sent into seclusion on Catalina Island to convert this material into conventional screenplay form.[8] With Ferguson gone from RKO, a new unit art director, Mark-Lee Kirk, was assigned. Stanley Cortez, a cameraman whose previous work had been almost exclusively in B pictures, was Welles's surprise choice. Mercury Theatre people were selected for some of the best roles (Joseph Cotten as Eugene Morgan, Agnes Moorehead as Aunt Fanny, Ray Collins as Jack Amberson), but there were some major surprises there, too — starlet Anne Baxter (she had a featured part in Jean Renoir's just-released *Swamp Water*) as Lucy, silent star Dolores Costello (former wife and costar of John Barrymore, she had been out of the limelight for years) as Isabel, and especially cowboy actor Tim Holt as George Minafer. Welles planned the film as a painstaking reconstruction of the turn-of-the-century milieu depicted in Tarkington's novel, with the Ambersons' elegant mansion as its visual center-piece. The ambitiousness of these production values was reflected in the preliminary budget estimate, which came to $987,024. For the third time, a Welles project was several hundred thousand dollars over a specified maximum. Schaefer quickly made his astonishment known to Welles.[9] Paring and trimming reduced that figure to $853,950. This was still well above both the limit in Welles's contract and the current ceiling on RKO productions, but somehow Welles managed to prevail on Schaefer once again, and Schaefer secured the necessary approval from his board.

Shooting began on October 28 at the RKO–Pathe lot in Culver City, where the entire Mercury operation had relocated to secure additional space for its expanded production schedule — and doubtless also to escape the many watchful eyes at the Gower Street operation. On November 28, Schaefer and Joe Breen (now RKO's West Coast head) were given a look at the work in progress. Three of the film's key sequences had been completed by then — the Ambersons' ball, the dinner at the Ambersons' for Eugene, and the encounter afterwards between George and Aunt Fanny on the hall staircase. These sequences represented the film's strongest features particularly well — its stunning sets and pictorial beauty, the technical virtuosity of the ballroom scenes, and the bravura performances of the Mercury Theatre players (especially of Agnes Moorehead). Both executives pronounced themselves delighted, and Schaefer's congratulatory message to Welles was full of glowing praise.[10]

At about this time, Welles was approached by the State Department's Committee on Inter-American affairs about making a film in South America as a goodwill gesture to promote hemispheric relations. Welles was being criticized at the time for his draft-exempt status, and the South American venture would give him an opportunity to enlist his talent in the service of a noble wartime cause. RKO was willing to cooperate, because the State Department would partly underwrite the project. The idea on which Welles settled was to make a South American version of *It's All True*. One episode would be based on the carnival in Rio. Since the carnival began in February, drastic changes would have to be made in Welles's other plans. As much would be finished on *The Magnificent Ambersons* as possible, and anything remaining would be supervised by Welles from a distance through an intermediary, Mercury business manager Jack Moss. The American *It's All True* would be scuttled, and Norman Foster (who was

Rehearsing the ballroom scene: Tim Holt, Anne Baxter, Ray Collins, and Richard Bennett.

already shooting the first episode, *My Friend Bonito,* in Mexico) would be reassigned to direct *Journey into Fear.*

Shooting on *The Magnificent Ambersons* was completed on January 22. Schaefer immediately let his West Coast people know he wanted the film ready in time for a major opening Easter week (one of the best times of the year for the movie business) at RKO's flagship theatre, Radio City Music Hall.[11] All deliberate speed was needed to make the target date. Wise quickly assembled a rough cut and flew with it to Miami in early February, where he and Welles screened it as Welles was passing through on his way to South America. Welles indicated what he wanted done and, just as he was boarding the plane for Rio, dictated a statement giving Wise full authority to act in his behalf.[12] Arrangements were undertaken to send Wise to Rio with the rough cut, but the plan fell through because of wartime travel restrictions. Wise proceeded as best he could and had a completed version of one hundred thirty-one minutes, forty-five seconds ready in early March. A print was shipped to Welles in Rio on March 11. Simultaneously, this version was put into preview.

The first preview, in Pomona, on March 17, was a disaster. This is how Schaefer described it to Welles:

Never in all my experience in the industry have I taken so much punishment or suffered as I did at the Pomona preview. In my 28 years in the business, I have never been present in a theatre where the audience acted in such a manner. They laughed at the wrong places, talked at the picture, kidded it, and did everything that you can possibly imagine.[13]

Wise did some quick patching on the most troublesome spots in time for a second preview, in Pasadena, on March 19. The reaction this time was better (a less rowdy audience, and only about a fourth of the preview cards were negative against three-fourths of the cards in Pomona), but there were still serious problems — the second half dragged badly and left some people confused, and certain scenes would not play. An impromptu committee of Wise, Joseph Cotten, and Moss worked out a strategy for reediting, but Welles rejected it out of hand.[14] The plan to send Wise to Rio was revived, but it failed to work out once again because of the war situation. Under the separate contract for *The Magnificent Ambersons* and *Journey into Fear*, RKO had the right to assume control of the editing after the first preview. After conferring with his legal department, Schaefer decreed that RKO would recut the film.

The task was entrusted to Wise, who was told to do whatever was necessary to get the film into releasable shape and given authority to act on his own. Excruciatingly detailed instructions continued to come from Welles via cable. Wise says he followed or accommodated these instructions wherever he could, but he himself made the final judgment. Working in consultation with Moss, Wise shortened a number of scenes, removed several others, and reshaped and reshot one scene. The ending was substantially revised and reshot by Freddie Fleck, the film's production manager. A new version of eighty-seven minutes was previewed to audiences in mid May to much more favorable reaction. One scene, however, continued to be especially troublesome, and it was now rewritten and reshot by Moss. A print incorporating this new footage was shipped to New York, and Schaefer made the final decisions. A version for release based on Schaefer's instructions with a running time of eighty-eight minutes, ten seconds was completed by Wise the first week in June.[15] Screenings for the press were held toward the end of the month. Most reviewers praised the film's artistic value, but the trade press judged it a hard sell. Meanwhile, Schaefer had been deposed as studio head, largely on account of Welles, and Welles himself would very shortly receive the ax. A new, tougher regime headed by Charles Koerner opened the film cautiously in other locations in advance of New York and, after what *Variety* called "spotty" results,[16] in effect abandoned it. It lost more than six hundred thousand dollars.

With *Greed*, an equally famous case, the issue was clear and simple: Von Stroheim made a very long and expensive film, and Irving Thalberg ordered it recut for commercial reasons and apparently with little remorse. With *The Magnificent Ambersons*, the situation is more complicated. All the evidence suggests that Schaefer intended to do everything he could for the film, but practical realities eventually forced his hand. The Music Hall opening indicates that he was prepared to go all out and that he was assuming that *The Magnificent Ambersons* could be promoted to a general audience. The combined experience of

Above, the Amberson's kitchen, a photograph from the set stills book. Below, on the veranda of the Ambersons' mansion, a scene deleted from the film.

Pomona and Pasadena effectively dashed that hope, and the improved reaction at an affluent and relatively highbrow place like Pasadena only served to confirm what eventually turned out to be true — that *The Magnificent Ambersons* was what in trade parlance is called a "special" picture. Nevertheless, that in itself was not the root cause of the problem. Films of this type could be promoted in ways that minimized the potential for loss. Instead, it was another complication that effectively sealed the film's fate. Closing figures revealed that *The Magnificent Ambersons* had gone drastically over budget — $1,013,760.46 in actual costs against an estimate of $853,950. As the smallest of the five major studios, RKO's distribution capacity was limited. Up to that time, no RKO release with a total picture cost in excess of one million dollars had ever realized a profit for the studio — not even major entertainment vehicles like *Carefree* or *Gunga Din*.[17] There was universal agreement that *The Magnificent Ambersons* required surgery of some type. Only Welles could do it and still preserve the film's artistic integrity. But with the production already beyond the fail-safe point, this would mean enormous additional expense, and there was not the slightest chance of recouping it. It would also have caused a long delay and heavy losses on the already troubled *It's All True,* which would probably have meant the end of that project, too. There was other gloomy news — *Journey into Fear* had gone considerably over budget, and *Citizen Kane* was completing its play-off without coming near breaking even. In the circumstances, Schaefer had little choice but to cut his losses.

In many respects, *Citizen Kane* is a model of economy in filmmaking. What happened to change things so radically on *The Magnificent Ambersons?* Welles himself provides the first clues. When Schaefer confronted him with the budgetary overrun, he attributed it to two things: illness and a "criminally slow cameraman."[18] Ray Collins contracted pneumonia after several days of shooting the snow scenes in an ice house and was out for ten days. Dolores Costello and Anne Baxter both missed several days later on because of illness.[19] In each case, the shooting schedule had to be rearranged, and this involved some additional expense. The problem with Stanley Cortez was much more serious. Welles thought he took too much time lighting and lining up shots. Welles wanted everything to be in clear and sharp focus, as it was in *Citizen Kane,* but Cortez was unable to achieve this to his satisfaction. The film was to contain a bravura shot in which the camera, as the eyes of George Minafer, moved around inside the deserted mansion — across the enormous reception hall, up and around the curving staircase, down the second-floor corridor, and into his mother's room. According to *Variety,* Cortez spent four days working out the mechanics of this shot.[20] Apparently the result failed to satisfy Welles — the footage does not appear in the cutting continuity for the early, uncut version. Although Cortez turned out some brilliant work — most notably in the ballroom and snow sequences — his successes tended to come at a very high price; shooting on the snow scenes, for instance, put the production several days behind schedule. The further along shooting went, the more the pace lagged. In the second month, several full working days were spent without a single scene's being completed. There were several contributing factors (like the extra rehearsal time needed for Tim Holt and Dolores Costello, who had more demanding roles than they were accustomed to), but Cortez's struggle with the technical requirements continued to be a major one. For instance, Costello needed special lighting and filters to mask the blemishes on her face. This was not an unusual problem for a Hollywood cameraman, but it gave Cortez a great deal of trouble. Wise says that, toward the end, Welles simply got rid of Cortez by demoting him to second unit work and replacing him with an RKO veteran, Harry Wild. When *The Magnificent Ambersons* officially closed on January 22 after seventy-six days of shooting, it was fourteen days behind schedule. Had it not been for stopgap measures toward the end — longer hours, the breakup into separate units, and one day of unscheduled work on Sunday — it would have been even farther behind. According to some who were on the set, Cortez was not particularly slow. The real problem was that he was not up to the technical extravagance of Welles's demands. In short (everyone present was acutely aware of the unspoken comparison), he was not Gregg Toland. Toland could be just as slow, but he always came through. Cortez's performance was intermittent.[21]

The budget figures provide additional clues. There were overruns in almost every category. One of the largest was for sound. Noises from the camera crane and other sources created problems for the original sound recording, and virtually the entire sound track had to be rerecorded on the dubbing stage. According to the rerecording engineer, Welles had been aware of the problems but went ahead anyway rather than sacrifice the camera effects he wanted.[22] The rerecording alone cost nearly twenty-five thousand dollars, almost three times what was budgeted. By far the largest share of the overage, however, came from the sets. The combined overrun for set construction, maintenance, labor, and striking and for props and drapery amounted to more than forty thousand dollars, roughly 25 percent of the total. The largest single expense in the budget by far was for set construction, $137,265.44. This is enormously expensive — as a percentage of total picture cost it is nearly twice the proportion for *Citizen Kane,* almost three times as much as *Gone With the Wind,* more even than RKO's all-time-champion set-centered film, *The Hunchback of Notre Dame.*[23]

The largest share of the set budget went for the interiors of the Ambersons' mansion. These were painstakingly reproduced from original historical models. (The source book was *Artistic Houses; Being a Series of Interior Views of a Number of the Most Beautiful and Celebrated Homes in the United States* — an outsized, profusely illustrated four-volume set published in a limited edition by D. Appleton in the 1880s.) Some of the results are strikingly beautiful, such as the entrance foyer, the dining room, and the staircase. However, several equally striking and costly sets saw only minimal use. During the ballroom sequence, there are lavishly designed and appointed sets that we glimpse only for seconds as the camera passes through them; we never see them again. The parlor where Wilbur Minafer lies in state is fully realized down to the tiniest detail, yet the scene is shot from the point of view of the coffin, and passing mourners block our view of most of the set. Two of the most lavish sets, the library and the drawing room, were used

Mark-Lee Kirk's elegant parlor set in the Ambersons' mansion dressed for Wilbur Minafer's lying-in-state. In the film, the scene is shot from the point of view of the coffin. In the lower left view, the cast and crew can be seen through the doorway in the center on an adjoining set. In the view above, the front entranceway can be seen in the distance.

for only one or two brief scenes. Clearly, Welles could have got by with a lot less. Nor are these sets particularly outstanding examples of set design. They represent the kind of expensive technical perfection that was the specialty of the Hollywood system; there were probably two dozen art directors who, given the same resources, could have done them just as well. Outstanding set design was what Perry Ferguson accomplished on *Citizen Kane* — delivering high value at a low price. It is not unreasonable to think that if some of the same budgetary constraints had been forced on *The Magnificent Ambersons,* not only might a considerable amount have been saved without appreciably compromising production values, but the film might also have benefited from the creative challenge, as *Citizen Kane* did. A profile of the eliminated footage suggests that these observations would not be contradicted by the long version of the film. Of the roughly forty-five minutes that were removed, only about a third involved the expensive Ambersons' interior sets — less than six minutes of the ballroom

sequences, five minutes on the second-floor hallway and rooms, and four minutes in the library and drawing room. Most of these reductions involve the shortening of extremely long takes of shots that remain in the release version. Nearly half of the forty-five-minute total involved three sets that no longer appear: The meeting room of a boys' club to which George belongs, a veranda of the Ambersons' mansion, and Fanny's boarding house. Surviving photographs indicate that all three sets were very modest and inexpensive.

Another budget detail stands out — not because of how large it is but because of how small. The cost of the screenplay is entered as fifteen hundred dollars. Welles received $50,000 for directing, plus a combined fee of $50,000 for producing and writing. The combined fee is entered only once, in the production category. To do the screenplay, Welles reverted to the method of *Heart of Darkness* — blocking out scenes in the original and turning this material over to Kent for conversion to standard form. Unlike *Heart of Darkness,* however, he later made very few changes. *The Magnificent Ambersons* is virtually unique in the Welles canon for its fidelity to its source. In the early parts, this is no problem. Welles's opening montage and chorus of townspeople, a telescoping of bits and pieces from the novel, is a master stroke, an ideal cinematic equivalent for Tarkington's old-fashioned scenic exposition. The ball and snow scenes are displays of technical virtuosity on the order of the publisher's party in *Citizen Kane.* After that, however, the story begins to flag. A large part of the problem lies with Welles's screenplay, which tends increasingly to become a succession of dialogue set pieces — in effect, a script for a radio show. The problem becomes more acute in the final third, in which a series of emotionally incandescent scenes documents the calamities that befall individual members of the Amberson clan. This part of the story is almost unrelievedly gloomy. As one member of the preview audience put it:

A very interesting picture to start with but the last reels and death scenes too draggy or prolonged. With a few changes it could be a fine picture. . . . As my mother says (and she is 77) don't bury the whole cast at once. Leave a few to be happy ever after.[24]

Besides pace and tone, there is also a problem of disconnectedness. Events that were widely separated in the novel come cascading one on top of another — Isabel dies, cut to the Major pondering eternity before his own death, cut to the revelation of Fanny's financial ruin, cut to George's desperate visit to lawyer Bronson, cut to Uncle Jack (now a bust, too) taking his final leave of George, cut to George's final walk home and his prayer kneeling over his mother's bed as the narrator intones solemn words about his comeuppance. The most extreme recutting took place in this section, as the scenes were shifted around in an effort to relieve the pace and conceal the absence of dramatic cohesion.[25] The ending caused the most trouble of all. In the novel, Eugene visits the hospital (Lucy and Fanny are already there), and he and George are reconciled. For some reason, Welles decided to eliminate the scene itself and to have Eugene write and narrate a letter to Isabel telling her about it. Besides the dramatic improbability, the narrative device had probably been used one time too many, and an alternate version was shot — Eugene visits Fanny at her boarding house, and they talk as her elderly companions look on. This sequence ran more than six minutes, and it was very downbeat. It was finally replaced by the present abbreviated meeting between Eugene and Fanny in the hospital corridor. The general assumption has been that the disconnected quality of the film that we have is a result of the reediting. Actually, a good deal of the problem appears to have been with the footage even before it was reedited, but not until the March previews did the problem come to light. Ironically, Welles's decision to dispense with the services of a screenwriting professional on *The Magnificent Ambersons* may have been the costliest misstep of all.

Where in the chain of causality was the crucial link? Was it when Welles failed to drop everything and rush home at the first sign of real danger? Was it when Wise was unable to get out of the country? Was it when Welles departed for South America leaving important creative business unfinished? Actually, we can go back much farther. The heart of the problem, I think, is in the production circumstances themselves. There was no screenwriter, and the art director and cinematographer were Welles's second choices. The production had major problems in all three areas. Collectively, these problems were enough to make the difference. If Welles had had the best talent available in these key roles — people who could meet his extraordinary demands while maintaining the kind of steady and efficient professional discipline that the production needed — *The Magnificent Ambersons* might have rivaled *Citizen Kane*. He had such collaborators on the earlier film. That is one major difference between not only *Citizen Kane* and *The Magnificent Ambersons* but between *Citizen Kane* and every other film Welles has made.

Citizen Kane is a major artistic achievement only partly because of Welles's intelligence and personal style. Much is also due to its screenplay, art direction, cinematography, special effects, music, and sound. I have had several conversations on this topic with Welles. The first time we met, in California in the summer of 1979, he spent almost the whole time regaling me with choice anecdotes about his father, Broadway, John Houseman, John Barrymore, and various film and literary figures. He was utterly charming, and I could see how he might have talked George Schaefer out of anything. The second day, he got directly down to business, asking what was in the notebooks I had with me (the illustrations for this book) and what was the theme of my book. When I began to throw out phrases like "filmmaking as a collaborative enterprise," I could see him glower, and after a while he could take no more. He exploded, and out came all his rancor over John Houseman and Pauline Kael and the Mankiewicz controversy, together with diatribes about the utter banality of most people working in Hollywood. Then there was a long, wistful meditation on his career — how he had started out wanting to be an American Charles Dickens, whether it would have been better if he had never left Broadway, how he only feels completely alive when he is engaged in film directing, how his most cherished project is a stark, black-and-white *King Lear* for television. Finally, after a long silence, he returned to our original subject with a simple and frank admission — his principal collaborators on *Citizen Kane* did indeed make extremely important contributions to the film. He singled out four: Herman Mankiewicz, Bernard Herrmann, and, most especially, Gregg Toland and Perry Ferguson. The first three were already familiar, but it was this conversation that first put me on the trail of Perry Ferguson's genuinely astonishing work on *Citizen Kane* and that ultimately helped to determine the final organization of this book.

I completed the part on Toland first and published it separately. I introduced it with a general statement about Welles and collaboration that described him as extremely ambivalent on the subject and that briefly summarized his reactions during our conversations in California. I sent him a copy. Shortly after, we had a long conversation by telephone. He disputed several minor points of interpretation in the body of the article, but in general he was very laudatory. He also volunteered new information that the article had brought to mind, and he made other helpful suggestions. The introduction was another matter. He was clearly upset with it, and I was treated to yet another display of Wellesian pique. But also once again he came directly and eloquently back to the point. He is most definitely not ambivalent on the subject of collaboration, he said, but has a clear-cut point of view. Collaborators make contributions, but only a director can make a film. He is the one element in the formula that cannot be sacrificed. Without him, *Citizen Kane* could not have been made. That, so far as he was concerned, was the real heart of the matter. I think there is no disputing Welles on this point. At the same time, I think it has a corollary. The quality of a film is partly a measure of the quality of its collaborative talent. On *Citizen Kane,* Welles was fortunate to have collaborators ideally suited to his temperament and working methods and capable of performing at his level of ambition. The film could never have been what it is without them. From the evidence of *Heart of Darkness* and *The Magnificent Ambersons* and the rest of Welles's career, I am willing to go further: Had it not been for this particular combination, we might not have *Citizen Kane* at all.

Appendix: Outtakes

Brothel Sequence: As originally written, the celebration party for the *Inquirer* staff was to have adjourned to a high-class brothel, Georgie's Place. After the Hays Office objected, the action was restructured so that girls like those at Georgie's became part of the chorus line at the *Inquirer* party. The brothel scenes were actually shot but not used. The photographs taken on the brothel set are from Joseph Cotten's notebooks in the Cinema Library, University of Southern California.

Above, the brothel sequence in rehearsal.

Above, with cigarette, playing Georgie, the madame, is Joan Blair, singer and girlfriend of bandleader Artie Shaw. Actress Frances Neal plays the girl paying special attention to Leland.

A sketch artist's treatment of the hospital roof set. The exaggerated depth perspective suggests that the artist is envisioning the set as it would appear to the 24 mm wide-angle lens. The set was not completed. After Welles sprained his ankle in shooting, Joseph Cotten and William Alland were brought in out of scheduled order to play the scenes against a blank screen, and the background was printed in later. The sketch is from the Maurice Zuberano collection, Film Study Center, Museum of Modern Art.

An unused treatment of the Great Hall set attributed to Allan Abbott. Baroque windows rise to Gothic points. The columns and vaulted ceilings in the loggia are vaguely Venetian. A military or heroic figure on a pedestal dominates the staircase. Are the caryatids supporting the fireplace mantel whimsical porcine figures or nude women?

SKETCHES OF DELETED SCENES

Following is a series of art department sketches of scenes in the script that were later eliminated.

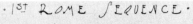

AS WRITTEN WORD 'ROME' TRAVELS ACROSS AND OFF OF SCREEN WE SEE

SHADOW OF HORSE DRAWING BAROUCHE COME ACROSS SCREEN FOLLOWED QUICKLY

BY THE CARRIAGE. AS THATCHER AND PARKER QUICKLY ALIGHT AND START

TOWARD US. CAMERA PULLS BACK AND SHOWS GRILLED DOORWAY THRU WHICH WE WERE LOOKING

HAND COME IN AND OPENS GRILLE FOLLOWING IMMEDIATE BY

SEE OTHER CARD FOR KANE'S DRAWING ROOM & SMALL EXQUISITE ROOM IN ROME

THE OPENING OF

A DOOR INTO ROOM AND THATCHER AND PARKER ARE ANNOUNCED

CAMERA PULLS BACK AS THEY WALK FORWARD TO

KANE AT FIRE PLACE

WHERE DIALOUGE TAKES PLACE AND A DISSOLVE SHOWS US

KANE, THATCHER AND POSSIBLY BERNSTEIN IN LIBRARY THAT NIGHT-WHEN DIALOUGE IS COMPLETED DISSOLVE

TO THATCHER SEATING HIM-SELF IN CARRIAGE AS IT PULLS OUT FOLLOWED BY

SHADOW AGAINST BLANK WALL WHICH IN TURN IS FOLLOWED BY WRITTEN

WORDS IN THATCHER'S MEMOIRS.

I had

Rome: Originally, the Thatcher manuscript contained an account of the financier's visit to Kane in Rome on his twenty-fifth birthday. Thatcher is accompanied by the American ambassador to Rome, Jefferson Parker. That evening, Kane and Thatcher meet in Kane's private quarters to discuss the future management of Kane's interests.

Kane's private quarters in Rome.

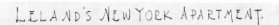

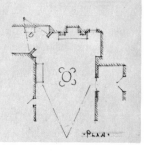

New York: (Pages 140–142.) The early scripts show how Kane and Leland as young singles in New York play as intently as they work. They are especially fond of the company of women of questionable morals. Kane frequents a high-class brothel, Georgie's Place.

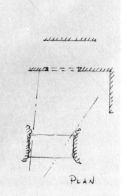

PLAN

INT. GEORGIE'S PLACE
(REPLACES "SMALL DINING ROOM)

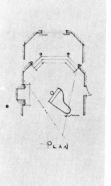

PLAN

CUNARD DOCKS

N ON PASSPORT OF KANE

AND PULL BACK SHOWING OFFICIAL CLOSING IT AND

HANDING IT TO KANE AND

CAMERA PULLS BACK TO INCLUDE BERNSTEIN AND LELAND - CONTINUE TO

TRAVEL BACK TO INCLUDE GANGPLANK ETC THEN FOLLOW THREE PRINCIPLES UP

TO GANGPLANK WHERE HALF-WAY UP BERNSTEIN AND LELAND ARE STOPPED BY 'ALL ABORE DOWN PLANK.

THEY SAY THEIR LAST GOOD BYE AND RETURN BACK DOWN PLANK.

NOTE: THIS IS ONE CONTINUOUS SHOT - NITE - RAIN-

Cunard Docks: When Kane leaves for Europe, Leland and Bernstein see him off.

HONEYMOON CAMP IN NORTH WOODS
(REVISED)

PACKAGE FROM TOWN, AS KANE FINISHES BUSINESS WITH THEM WE SHOOT

FROM UNDER PORCH OF KANE'S TENT AS HE FINDS ARTICLE OF INTEREST-END OF DIALOGUE WE DISSOLVE.

TO INSIDE OF TENT, SHOWING KANE'S SILHOUETTE, READING, AS EMILY WALKS INTO SHOT, STANDS AT DOOR WATCHING.

LONG SHOT OF CAMP SET UP AT NATURAL LOCATION CHEFS, FIRES, SERVANTS ETC AND MEN COMING WITH

ALTERNATE SHOT FOR NUMBER 4 ABOVE

PLAN IS SELF EXPLANATORY

Wisconsin Honeymoon: An enormous retinue accompanies Kane and Emily on their honeymoon in the North Woods. The future rift in their marriage is foreshadowed as Kane is unable to keep his mind off business matters.

White House: An item in a newspaper tips Kane off to the sale of leases that will culminate in a scandal like Teapot Dome, and he interrupts his honeymoon to go to Washington to confront the president.

First Marriage: Kane and Emily at home circa 1900. For economy reasons, only the background set, the breakfast room, was actually built.

Yacht Cruise: Kane arranges for Susan's young lover at Xanadu to have a fatal "accident," then takes her away on an extended around-the-world cruise.

Chapel at Xanadu: Howard, Kane's son from his marriage with Emily, is killed when he and other members of a fascist organization try to seize an armory in Washington. He is buried in the chapel at Xanadu near his paternal grandmother. The verse inscription on the wall is from *1001 Nights* and begins, "The drunkenness of youth has passed like a fever."

Production Credits

Production	A Mercury Theatre Production for RKO Radio Pictures (Academy Award Nomination, Best Picture)
Producer	Orson Welles
Associate Producer	Richard Baer
Assistants	William Alland, Richard Wilson
Direction	Orson Welles (AAN)
Assistant Directors	Eddie Donahoe, Freddie Fleck
Screenplay	Original Screenplay by Herman J. Mankiewicz and Orson Welles (Academy Award)
Editorial Supervision	John Houseman
Script Continuity and Supervision	Amalia Kent
Cinematography	Gregg Toland, ASC (AAN)
Camera Operator	Bert Shipman
Gaffer	Bill McClellan
Grip	Ralph Hoge
Assistant Cameraman	Eddie Garvin
Early Makeup and Wardrobe Tests	Russell Metty
Retakes and Additional Shooting	Harry Wild
Art Direction	Van Nest Polglase, Head of Department
Art Director	Perry Ferguson
Assistant	Hilyard Brown
Principal Sketch Artist	Charles Ohmann
Sketches and Graphics	Al Abbott, Claude Gillingwater, Jr., Albert Pyke, Maurice Zuberano

Set Decorations

Darrell Silvera (AAN), Head
of Department

Assistant .... Al Fields

Prop Manager .... Charles Sayers

Costumes .... Edward Stevenson

Wardrobe .... Earl Leas, Margaret Van Horn

Makeup .... Mel Berns, Head of Department

Makeup Artist .... Maurice Seiderman

Assistant .... Layne (Shotgun) Britton

Special Effects .... Vernon L. Walker, Head of Department

Optical Printing .... Linwood G. Dunn

Effects Cameraman .... Russell Cully

Montage Effects .... Douglas Travers

Matte Artist .... Mario Larrinaga

Editing .... Robert Wise (AAN)

Assistant .... Mark Robson

"News on the March" ..... RKO Newsreel Department

Sound Recording .... John Aalberg (AAN), Head of Department

Production Mixer .... Bailey Fesler

Boom .... Jimmy Thompson

Rerecording .... James G. Stewart

Special Sound Effects .... Harry Essman

Music

Composer, Orchestrator,
Conductor, Recording Supervisor ..... Bernard Herrmann (AAN)

"News on the March" Music ..... Taken from the scores of earlier RKO
releases — *Abe Lincoln in Illinois*
(1940), *Bad Lands* (1939), *Bringing Up
Baby* (1938), *The Conquerors* (1932),
Curtain Call (1940), *Five Came Back*
(1939), *The Flying Irishman* (1939),
Gunga Din (1939), *A Man to Remember*
(1938), *Mother Carey's Chickens*
(1938), *Music for Madame* (1937),
Nurse Edith Cavell (1939), *On Again,
Off Again* (1937), and *Reno* (1939);
orchestrations of familiar works
("Tannhauser," "Chopin Funeral

March," and so on) as they were scored
for those films

"Charlie Kane" Song
    Lyrics   Herman Ruby
    Vocalization   Charles Bennett
    Choreography of dance number   Arthur Appel

Mercury Theatre Publicist   Herbert Drake

Still Photographer   Alex Kahle

Notes

Notes to Preface

1. Roy Fowler, *Orson Welles: A First Biography* (London: Pendulum, 1946); *Citizen Kane* part reprinted in *Focus on "Citizen Kane,"* ed. Ronald Gottesman (Englewood Cliffs, N.J.: Prentice-Hall, 1971), 89.

2. Pauline Kael, "Raising Kane," *The New Yorker,* February 20, 1971, 43–89, and February 27, 1971, 44–81; reprinted as the introduction to *The "Citizen Kane" Book* (Boston: Little, Brown, 1971), 1–84; softcover edition, New York: Bantam, 1974, 1–124. The Little Brown edition will be cited. A typical reply is Joseph McBride's "Rough Sledding with Pauline Kael," *Film Heritage* 7, no. 1 (Fall 1971): 13–16, 32.

3. James Naremore, *The Magic World of Orson Welles* (New York: Oxford University Press, 1978), 65. I treat the developments mentioned in my opening paragraph in the last section of Chapter Five.

4. Charles Higham, *The Films of Orson Welles* (Berkeley: University of California Press, 1970), 9–47.

5. Peter Bogdanovich, "The Kane Mutiny," *Esquire,* October 1972, 99–105, 180–90.

6. Joseph McBride, *Orson Welles* (New York: Viking, 1972), 7–51.

7. Donald W. Rea, "A Critical-Historical Account of the Planning, Production, and Release of *Citizen Kane,*" unpublished master's thesis, University of Southern California, 1966.

Notes to Chapter One

1. In final form, it was actually three contracts: a production agreement between RKO and the Mercury Theatre, under which Welles, acting for the Mercury corporation, would produce, direct, and write the screenplay for two pictures, at $70,000 for the first and $90,000 for the second; an employment agreement between RKO and Welles as an actor, to perform the leading male role in two pictures, at $30,000 plus 20 percent of the profits for the first and $35,000 plus 25 percent for the second; and a guarantee agreement between RKO and Welles as an individual obligating him to render the services called for in the production agreement to the Mercury. The first picture was to be completed by January 1, 1940, the second sometime during 1940. The contracts were subsequently redrawn several times as Welles went beyond deadlines or changed his plans.

2. The fullest account of the Schaefer era at RKO is in Richard B. Jewell's unpublished Ph.D. thesis, "A History of RKO Radio Pictures, Incorporated, 1928–1942" (University of Southern California, 1978), 466–727. A condensed version appears in *The RKO Story,* by Richard B. Jewell with Vernon Harbin (New York: Arlington House, 1982). A good

contemporary summary of Schaefer's career is given in *International Motion Picture Alma-nac, 1941–42*, ed. Terry Ramsaye (New York: Quigley, 1942), 558.

3. *Hollywood Reporter,* September 26, 1939, p. 1.

4. The main story documents surviving from the *Heart of Darkness* project and listed here are titled as are the originals. Page totals given here (and throughout) are the actual number of pages; because of revisions, the paginations on the scripts themselves are often arbitrary. Documents surviving are: pasteups of the source novel, edited and annotated by Welles (Mercury; a note in the files by Richard Wilson, their longtime curator, indicates that Welles's copy of a subsequent script draft with his notes and sketches was borrowed by Peter Bogdanovich and not returned); "Story Outline," September 1, 1939, 31 pp., apparently by Welles; "Index to List of Characters," undated, 44 pp., apparently by Welles; "Heart of Darkness" [Story synopsis], September 15, 1939, 2 pp., probably for use in publicity (Mer-cury); "First Rough Draft Estimating Script," November 7, 1939, 202 pp., the continuity script prepared by Kent from Welles's draft; "Revised Estimating Script," November 21, 1939, 192 pp., extensively annotated concerning the shooting of special effects; "Re-hearsal Script," November 27, 1939, 60 pp., from Marlow's arrival at the First Station to the incident of the snake, probably used in the test shooting; and "Revised Estimating Script," November 30, 1939, 189 pp. The prologue photograph used here is from the Mer-cury collection. The art department sketches are from the collection of John Mansbridge. The photographs of set models are courtesy of Ron Haver. The script of the prologue sequence, with a commentary by Jonathan Rosenbaum, "The Voice and the Eye," was published in *Film Comment* 8, no. 4 (November–December 1972): 24–32. Hubert Cohen has considered the carryover of "The *Heart of Darkness* in *Citizen Kane*" in *Cinema Jour-nal* 12, no. 1 (Fall 1972): 11–25.

5. Joseph Conrad, *Heart of Darkness,* ed. Robert Kimbrough (New York: W. W. Nor-ton, 1963), 5.

6. J. R. McDonough to Schaefer, December 18, 1939.

7. [Story synopsis], September 15, 1939.

8. Welles received a special award from TWA as its best customer of 1939. According to the airline, he flew 311,425 miles on round trips between Los Angeles and New York. *Hollywood Reporter,* April 5, 1940, 4.

9. Schaefer to Welles, November 16, 1939.

10. Interview with Linwood Dunn, July 11, 1978.

11. Interview with Amalia Kent, September 13, 1983.

12. McDonough to Schaefer, December 7, 1939.

13. Schaefer to J. J. Nolan, December 11, 1939.

14. Leah Josephson, "Story Synopsis," November 1, 1939.

15. The postponement was announced in *Hollywood Reporter,* January 13, 1940, 3. Three main scripts survive: "First Rough Draft Continuity and Treatment," December 12, 1939, 145 pp., fragment with 7 pp. synopsis of rest of story, probably the version given to Carole Lombard; "First Rough Draft," December 26, 1939, 231 pp. (Mercury); and "Re-vised Estimating Script," January 9, 1940, 174 pp. Joseph Breen of the Production Code Office approved the "Revised Estimating Script" with minor exceptions on January 12. A preliminary budget estimate of $494,125 was issued on January 19.

16. *Variety,* September 27, 1939, 4.

17. Nolan to Schaefer, December 12, 1939.

18. *Hollywood Reporter,* January 8, 1940, 2.

Notes to Chapter Two

1. There are seven drafts of the *Citizen Kane* script in the RKO files: *American,* "First Rough Draft," April 16, 1940, 268 pp.; *Orson Welles #3,* "First Draft Continuity," May 9,

1940, 310 pp., inserted revisions dated April 30 to May 14; *Orson Welles #3,* "Second Draft Continuity," May 16, 1940, 245 pp., revisions dated May 17 to June 15; *Citizen Kane,* "Final," June 18, 1940, 209 pp., with changes of June 18 and 19; "Revised Final," June 24, 1940, 183pp., changes to July 2; "Second Revised Final," July 9, 1940, 168 pp.; and "Third Revised Final," July 16, 1940, 172 pp., with change of July 19. For a full history, see my "The Scripts of *Citizen Kane," Critical Inquiry* 5, no. 2 (Winter 1978): 369–400; portions of this chapter are condensed from that article.

2. One is *John Meade's Woman* (1937), the story of a lumber tycoon, which starred Edward Arnold. It contains a few superficial parallels with *Citizen Kane,* such as a scene at the Chicago Opera House and a chance meeting in the street between Arnold and a young girl that leads to further involvement, but it is otherwise uninteresting as a film. The authorized biography is Richard Meryman's *Mank: The Wit, World, and Life of Herman Mankiewicz* (New York: Morrow, 1978).

3. Kael, "Raising Kane," reprinted in *The "Citizen Kane" Book,* 34–35.

4. John Houseman, *Run-Through: A Memoir* (New York: Simon and Schuster, 1972), 444.

5. Affidavit of Richard Baer, May 1941 (Mercury).

6. Houseman, *Run-Through,* 445–61.

7. Kael, "Raising Kane," reprinted in *The "Citizen Kane" Book,* 35, 82–83.

8. Bogdanovich, "The Kane Mutiny," 180–82, 188.

9. [Robert Tallman], "Third Rehearsal Script: 'March of Time'," December 3, 1936.

10. This part is probably inspired by the Thomas Ince affair, but it is treated here along the lines of *After Many a Summer Dies the Swan*: In both versions, the affair goes on right at the castle, the old man takes matters into his own hands when he learns of it, and an employee helps to arrange a cover-up.

11. Ferdinand Lundberg, *Imperial Hearst* (New York: Equinox, 1936), 103.

12. *Lundberg* v. *Welles et al.* (transcripts in the Federal Records Center, Bayonne, New Jersey). Mankiewicz was a very uncooperative witness. Houseman also testified. Welles sent a deposition from Morocco. Lundberg's case was strong enough that the trial ended in a hung jury, and RKO settled out of court. For evidence of similar borrowing from other Hearst sources, for instance, Mrs. Fremont Older's *William Randolph Hearst, American* (New York: D. Appleton-Century, 1936), see my "Scripts of *Citizen Kane,*" 378–85.

13. It was commonly thought by those who worked on the film that a kind of ultimate transgression was involved in the depiction of Kane's death — a subject Hearst forbade mention of in his presence. Actually, Hearst had nullified this prohibition himself at the time the script was being written in Victorville. "Many of those who attended the Hearst birthday celebration over the weekend believed that 'W. R.' told them goodbye in his speech at Sunday's dinner. Although seemingly in the best of health, this grand journalist, who has spent most of his 76 years fighting, talked for the first time of death in addressing the members of his family and the Hearst organization who sat in on his birthday party. It is reported that there was not a dry eye among the 75 persons at the table after the head of the Hearst domain finished his brilliant talk." *Hollywood Reporter,* April 30, 1940, 2.

14. Second supplemental agreements, May 28, 1940.

15. Interview with Darrell Silvera, March 30, 1983.

16. McDonough to Schaefer, June 18, 1940.

17. In the interval, Mankiewicz had written a first draft of *Comrade X* for MGM. He received no screen credit or other recognition, and for several decades his work on the film remained a secret of the MGM files. He had also continued to involve himself in the *Citizen Kane* scripting. Early in June, after he had been off the payroll for weeks, he submitted a partial revised script of 137 pages that he had apparently worked out on his own (copy in the Mercury Collection). However, this document appears not to have been used. At about this time, Mankiewicz got hold of a copy of Welles's draft and sent it with complaints to Houseman in New York. Houseman replied that he liked most of Orson's new scenes. (Houseman to Mankiewicz, night letter, June 16, 1940, reprinted in "Scripts of *Citizen Kane,*" 394).

18. I am grateful to Professor Michael Ogden, author of a forthcoming book on Welles's work in radio, for verifying this information for me.

19. Weissberger to Welles, September 6, 1940 (Mercury).

20. Weissberger to Ross Hastings, October 1, 1940.

21. Hastings to Weissberger, October 3, 1940. For the record, Hastings explained that, until a few months previous, arbitrations over writer credits were conducted by Screen Playwrights, Inc., under a February 10, 1937, agreement between that organization and the Producers' Guild. That agreement had been terminated. In the interim, cases of arbitration were being handled by the Screen Writers' Guild, but only with the prior consent of all the writers involved. The new agreement with the Screen Writers' Guild would not go into effect until October 10, 1940. Even apart from the contracts technicality, then, Mankiewicz would not be able to force an arbitration, because there was no established jurisdiction.

22. *Hollywood Reporter,* October 3, 1940, 2.

23. After *Citizen Kane* had been completed, someone at RKO drew up an information sheet on the persons involved that summarized their functions. Mankiewicz is listed as writer (but not Welles), with the following notation: "Mr. Mankiewicz was the principal writer — in fact wrote the screen play about which there was considerable discussion as to his right to receive screen credit." "*Citizen Kane* [Personnel List]," [January 1941?].

24. Dore Schary to Mercury Productions, January 18, 1941.

25. Welles and Mankiewicz, Request to the Screen Writers' Guild, January 22, 1941.

26. Morris Cohn to Welles and Mankiewicz, January 30, 1941.

27. Kael, "Raising Kane," reprinted in *The "Citizen Kane" Book,* 38.

28. Welles, "The Creation of *Citizen Kane,*" *London Times,* November 17, 1971, 17.

29. Welles, deposition in *Lundberg v. Welles et al.,* taken by Walter S. Blair, Casablanca, Morocco, May 4, 1949, 20–21.

Notes to Chapter Three

1. For the detailed portrait of the old RKO art department given in this chapter, I am especially indebted to three of its former employees: Hilyard Brown, a set designer, Perry Ferguson's chief assistant on *Citizen Kane,* and a leading art director today; John Mansbridge, apprentice set designer, now head of the art department at Walt Disney Studios; and Maurice Zuberano, a sketch artist, now a production illustrator who works most often with Robert Wise. Also see Edward Carrick, *Designing for Films,* rev. ed. (London: Studio, 1949), especially 48–50; Léon Barsacq, *Caligari's Cabinet and Other Grand Illusions: A History of Film Design,* rev. and ed. Elliott Stein, trans. Michael Bullock (Boston: Little, Brown, 1976), especially Stein's "Filmographies of Art Directors and Production Designers"; Ellen Spiegel, "Fred and Ginger Meet Van Nest Polglase," *The Velvet Light Trap,* no. 10 (Fall 1973): 17–22 and Zuberano's letter of reply in *The Velvet Light Trap,* no. 11 (Spring 1974): 47; and Norman Paul Gambill, "*Citizen Kane:* An Art Historical Analysis," unpublished Ph.D. thesis (Syracuse University, 1976), 153–83, 251–84.

2. Richard B. Jewell with Vernon Harbin, *The RKO Story* (New York: Arlington House, 1982), 101, 128.

3. For background information on the production difficulties of these three films, see Jewell, *The RKO Story* and the fuller accounts in the dissertation that was its source, Jewell's "A History of RKO Radio Pictures, Incorporated, 1928–1942."

4. For the record, the unit art directors in RKO's heyday from the middle thirties to the early forties included, besides Ferguson, Carroll Clark (best known for the Rogers–Astaire productions), Mark–Lee Kirk (formerly with D. W. Griffith; *The Informer, Kitty Foyle, The Magnificent Ambersons*), Al Herman (*King Kong* — with Clark, *Love Affair, The Hunchback of Notre Dame*), and Al D'Agostino (*The Devil and Miss Jones*), who replaced Polglase as department head in 1942. Allan Abbott and Charles Ohmann were the chief

sketch artists. Abbott's specialty was modern sets (for the Rogers–Astaire films, for instance). Ohmann worked on everything, but he was especially good on historical and period material. Other sketch artists on the payroll at the time of *Citizen Kane* were Albert Pyke, Claude Gillingwater, Jr., and Zuberano. The head draftsman was Charles Pyke. Working under him as set designers were Brown, Robert Cassiday, William Grau, John R. Kibbey, and Mansbridge.

5. They have been hole punched and bound together with a wire clasp fastener. *J. R. McDonough* is handwritten on the paper cover. They were probably collected for the front office in connection with the budgetary crisis. That they are unusual is underlined by the fact that in the entire business archive there are materials like these for only two films, *Citizen Kane* and a B western.

6. All are on Triple S-S-S shield mat board. Four are storyboards drawn in charcoal directly on the mat board: A twenty-by-thirty-inch board contains fifteen separate frames; another twenty-by-thirty-inch board contains fourteen frames; a fifteen-by-twenty-inch board contains eight frames; and another fifteen-by-twenty-inch board contains four frames. The other three are charcoal sketches — one eight-and-a-half-by-eleven-inch sketch drawn directly on a fifteen-by-twenty-inch mat board; one nine-by-twelve-inch sketch on artist's oil paper that has been taped to a fifteen-by-twenty-inch mat board with masking tape; and one ten-by-thirteen-inch sketch on artist's oil paper taped to a fifteen-by-twenty-inch mat board. Some of the material from this collection has been published by John Tibbetts, "*Citizen Kane* on the Drawing Board," *American Classic Screen* 2, no. 6 (July–August 1978): 32–39.

7. "Outline of Estimating Script," May 22, 1940.

8. "Hearst at Home," *Fortune*, May 1931, 56–68, 130. This article was probably one of Mankiewicz's sources; it is filled with numerous private details of the sort that are in the script — for instance, that a rented warehouse in New York City was filled with Hearst's things.

9. William J. Anderson, *The Architecture of the Renaissance in Italy*, 5th ed. (London: Batsford, 1927), plate 73. This book, along with about two dozen other volumes from the RKO art department library, is now interfiled with the working library of DeForest Research, a free-lance operation housed on the old RKO section of the Paramount lot.

10. Welles continued to insist that the Great Hall had to be an all-live-action set right up to the end of production. During the last week of shooting, he ordered one of the walls to be built higher (in place of the matte shot called for in the budget) in order to accommodate a moving camera shot that he and Toland had planned (Art Department Set Overage Report, October 17, 1940).

11. A matte painting with these details appears briefly in one shot in the sequence at the end with the reporters.

12. Each of these pieces would have been personally selected by Darrell Silvera, the head set decorator. Well-known in Hollywood for his skills as a decorator and for his expertise in antiques and art objects, Silvera was involved in decorating Marion Davies's beach house at Santa Monica. He denies ever intending to make fun of Hearst and Davies in the film, but his remarks about them in our conversations provide cause for wonder. When I asked him if he thought Hearst had any taste in art, he replied that he didn't know anything about that, but he did know Hearst had a lot of ugly furniture he wouldn't have in his own house. He tells of making oilcloth curtains for the beach house because the sea air kept soiling the fabric ones and of Davies's reaction. She loved them, he says, but he adds that, of course, they were awful. Silvera's reluctance to discuss Hearst in connection with the film may be a holdover from the original conspiracy of silence.

13. *Citizen Kane* Budget Detail, June 27, 1940.

14. *Hollywood Reporter*, September 3, 1940, 2.

15. *Citizen Kane* Souvenir Program, reprinted in *Souvenir Programs of Twelve Classic Movies 1927–1941*, ed. Miles Kreuger (New York: Dover, 1977), 217–36.

16. Welles to Schaefer, February 13, 1941.

17. Schaefer to McDonough, February 18, 1941.

18. Ferguson died in 1963. The credits for later films listed in Barsacq belong to Perry Ferguson, Jr.

19. Perry Ferguson, "More Realism from 'Rationed' Sets?" *American Cinematographer* 23, no. 9 (September 1942): 390–91, 430. The lesson was put into practice most effectively at RKO in the Val Lewton unit; see, for instance, the tower sequence in *I Walked with a Zombie.*

Notes to Chapter Four

1. For much of the detailed technical information in this chapter, I am indebted to Ralph Hoge, longtime member of Toland's camera crew and his key grip on *Citizen Kane.* Hoge and I screened a 35mm print of *Citizen Kane* on a Steenbeck viewing table at the UCLA Film Archive, stopping the action at appropriate points to discuss how the effects were achieved. On Toland's career, see George Mitchell, "A Great Cameraman," *Films in Review* 7, no. 10 (December 1956): 504–12; "Gregg Toland," *Sequence,* no. 8 (Summer 1949): 67–76 (a memorial tribute that includes a letter from William Wyler and an assessment, "The Work of Gregg Toland," by Douglas Slocombe); *Film Comment* 8, no. 2 (Summer 1972): 56 (filmography); and Roger D. Wallace, "Gregg Toland — His Contributions to Cinema," unpublished Ph.D. thesis (University of Michigan, 1976), and "Through a Lens Deeply: Gregg Toland as a Creator of Psychological Nuances," *Film/Psychology Review* 4, no. 2 (Summer–Fall 1980): 283–95. Discussions of Toland's contributions to *Citizen Kane* can be found in Higham, *The Films of Orson Welles,* 11–13; Kael, "Raising Kane,"reprinted in *The "Citizen Kane" Book,* 75–79; Bogdanovich, "The Kane Mutiny," 182–88; Patrick Ogle, "Technological and Aesthetic Influences upon the Development of Deep-Focus Cinematography in the United States," *Screen* 13, no. 1 (Spring 1972): 45–72; and Naremore, *The Magic World of Orson Welles,* 40–53. Toland wrote about his work on *Citizen Kane* in "Realism for *Citizen Kane,*" *American Cinematographer* 22, no. 2 (February 1941): 54–55, 80 and "How I Broke the Rules in *Citizen Kane,*" *Popular Photography,* June 1941, 55 (reprinted in Gottesman, ed., *Focus on "Citizen Kane,"* 73–77); see also his "Using Arcs for Lighting Monochrome," *American Cinematographer* 22, no. 12 (December 1941): 558–59, 588. On *The Long Voyage Home* as an adaptation, see John Orlandello, *O'Neill on Film* (Rutherford, N.J.: Fairleigh Dickinson, 1982), 89–102. This chapter was originally published in slightly different form as "Orson Welles and Gregg Toland: Their Collaboration on *Citizen Kane,*" *Critical Inquiry* 8, no. 4 (Summer 1982): 651–74.

2. Robert Wise in "*Citizen Kane* Remembered," *Action!* 4, no. 3 (May–June 1969): 31.

3. I examined this projection room in 1977, when it was still in use on the Paramount lot. The area it occupied has since been remodeled for office space.

4. Hoge in "*Citizen Kane* Remembered," 28.

5. Toland, "How I Broke the Rules," in *Focus on "Citizen Kane,"* 73–74.

6. This and the following paragraph are summarized from Ogle, "Technological and Aesthetic Influences." See also Wyler's letter in *Sequence,* no. 8 (Summer 1949); Slocombe, "The Work of Gregg Toland"; and Toland, "Realism for *Citizen Kane*" and "How I Broke the Rules."

7. See H. Mario Raimondo Souto, *Technique of the Motion Picture Camera,* 3d ed. (New York: Hastings House, 1977), 76–77. Souto implies that the first BNCs went to Warner Brothers. The Mitchell camera people tell me that the first two, BNC1 and BNC2, went to Samuel Goldwyn in 1934 and 1935. Only fifteen more BNCs were placed in service before 1940, when their manufacture was halted for the duration of the war. See also Ogle, "Technological and Aesthetic Influences," 59, and Mitchell, "A Great Cameraman," 508.

8. Mitchell, "A Great Cameraman," 508. For a catalogue of such devices, see Wallace, "Through a Lens Deeply," 284–86.

9. Toland, "Realism for *Kane*," 54.

10. John Chapman, *New York Daily News,* April 15, 1941.

11. Welles to Schaefer, March 3, 1941.

12. Reginald Armour to Walter Daniels, July 14, 1941.

13. Thomas Schatz, *Hollywood Genres: Formulas, Filmmaking, and the Studio System* (New York: Random House, 1981), 111–23; also see Foster Hirsch, *The Dark Side of the Screen* (South Brunswick, N.J.: A. S. Barnes, 1981), 121–24.

14. George Cukor, quoted in Gavin Lambert, *On Cukor* (New York: Putnam, 1972), 186.

15. Slocombe, "The Work of Gregg Toland," 74.

Notes to Chapter Five

1. Information in this chapter is based on interviews by the author with Linwood Dunn (July 11, 1978), James G. Stewart (July 10, 1978), and Robert Wise (July 18, 1978, and November 14, 1983).

Other interviews with Dunn can be found in Donald Chase, *Filmmaking: The Collaborative Art* (Boston: Little, Brown, 1975), 292–97 and in William Luhr and Peter Lehman, *Wide Angle* 1, no. 1 rev. and exp. (1979): 78–83. Relevant articles by Dunn: "Optical Printing and Technique," *American Cinematographer* 14, no. 11 (March 1934): 444–46, 470–71; "Tricks by Optical Printing," *American Cinematographer* 14, no. 12 (April 1934): 487, 496; "Optical Printing and Technic," *Journal of the Society of Motion Picture Engineers* 26 (January 1936): 54–66; "Optical Printer Handy Dandy," *International Photographer,* June 1938, 14, 16; and "The New Acme-Dunn Optical Printer," *Journal of the Society of Motion Picture Engineers* 42 (March 1944): 204–10. Also see "R-K-O Trick Departments Consolidated," *American Cinematographer* 13, no. 6 (October 1932): 45; Vernon L. Walker, "Use of Miniatures in Process Backgrounds," *American Cinematographer* 15, no. 4 (August 1934): 154, 162; "Special Effects at R.K.O.," *International Photographer,* December 1940, 4; Fred M. Sersen, "Special Photographic Effects," *Journal of the Society of Motion Picture Engineers* 40 (June 1943): 374–79; Walter Blanchard, "Unseen Camera-Aces II: Linwood Dunn, A.S.C.," *American Cinematographer* 24, no. 7 (July 1943): 254, 268, 270; "The Acme-Dunn Optical Printer," *International Photographer,* March 1944, 18; Raymond Fielding, *The Technique of Special Effects Cinematography,* 3d ed. (New York: Hastings House, 1972); Ron Fry and Pamela Fourzon, *The Saga of Special Effects* (Englewood Cliffs, N.J.: Prentice Hall, 1977), 86–88; and Ronald Haver, *David O. Selznick's Hollywood* (New York: Knopf, 1980), 76–87, 100–119. The matte paintings illustrated here are from Dunn's private collection. The background painting of Xanadu is from the collection of John Mansbridge.

For Stewart, also see "Development of Sound Technique," an American Film Institute/Louis B. Mayer Foundation Oral History, James G. Stewart interviewed by Irene Kahn Atkins, April 11–June 20, 1976 (Glen Rock, N.J.: Microfilming Corporation of America, 1977) and Stewart's article, "The Evolution of Cinematic Sound: A Personal Report," in *Sound and the Cinema,* ed. Evan William Cameron (Pleasantville, N.Y.: Redgrave, 1980), 38–67. On sound, see L. T. Goldsmith, "Rerecording Sound Motion Pictures," *The Technique of Motion Picture Production,* Society of Motion Picture Engineers, ed., (New York: Interscience Publishers, 1944), 43–49; Phyllis Goldfarb, "Orson Welles's Use of Sound," *Take One* 3, no. 6 (July–August 1971): 10–11; and Evan William Cameron, "*Citizen Kane:* The Influence of Radio Drama on Cinematic Design," in Cameron, ed., *Sound and the Cinema,* 202–16.

For Wise, also see his contribution to the "*Citizen Kane* Remembered" feature in *Action!* 4, no. 3 (May–June 1969): 31–32; an interview by Rui Nogueira, "Robert Wise at RKO," *Focus on Film* no. 12 (Winter 1972): 43–50; an American Film Institute Seminar, "Dialogue on Film: Robert Wise," *American Film* 1, no. 2 (November 1975): 33–48; brief interview remarks and a filmography, "As the Editor, You're the Audience," *Film Com-*

ment 13, no. 2 (March–April 1977): 21; and Samuel Stark, "Robert Wise," *Films in Review* 14, no. 1 (January 1963): 5–22.

2. Vernon Walker to McDonough and Sid Rogell, December 13, 1940.

3. Dunn, "Optical Printing and Technique," 444.

4. Chase, *Filmmaking*, 297.

5. Higham, *The Films of Orson Welles*, 13.

6. Interview with John Mansbridge, March 28, 1983.

7. McDonough to Schaefer, December 18, 1940.

8. Baer to Dan Winkler, October 17, 1940.

9. James Stewart, letter to the author, July 29, 1979.

10. Bernard Herrmann, "Score for a Film" (*New York Times*, May 25, 1941), reprinted in *Focus on "Citizen Kane*," 69. Also see, by Herrmann, "The Contemporary Use of Music in Film: *Citizen Kane, Psycho, Fahrenheit 451*," *University Film Study Center Newsletter 7*, no. 3 (February 1977): 5–10 and a longer version of the same piece lacking the question-and-answer transcript and bibliography, "Bernard Herrmann, Composer," in Cameron, ed., *Sound and the Cinema*, 117–35; and two interviews, both with Ted Gilling, "The Colour of the Music," *Sight and Sound* 41, no. 1 (Winter 1971–1972): 36–39, and "[On] *The 'Citizen Kane' Book*," *Sight and Sound* 41, no. 2 (Spring 1972): 71–73.

On the score of *Citizen Kane*, see Irene Kahn Atkins, *Source Music in Motion Pictures* (Rutherford, N.J.: Fairleigh Dickinson, 1983), 84–89; Jay Bartush, "*Citizen Kane*: The Music," *Film Reader* (Northwestern), no. 1 (1975): 50–54; Bogdanovich, "The Kane Mutiny," 181; Graham Bruce, *Bernard Herrmann: Film Music and Film Narrative* (Ann Arbor: University Microfilms International, 1983), 101–25; Higham, 14–17; and Christopher Palmer, liner notes for "*Citizen Kane*: The Classic Film Scores of Bernard Herrmann" (New York: RCA Records ARL 1–0707, 1974). Kathryn Kalinak's unpublished essay, "A Study in Collaboration: *The Magnificent Ambersons* of Orson Welles and Bernard Herrmann," is summarized in *Quarterly Review of Film Studies* 6, no. 4 (Fall 1981): 459.

Also see Royal S. Brown, "Herrmann, Hitchcock, and the Music of the Irrational," *Cinema Journal* 21, no. 2 (Spring 1982): 14–49; Page Cook, "Bernard Herrmann," *Films in Review* 18, no. 7 (August–September 1967): 398–412 (also the correspondence on this article in *Films in Review* 18, no. 8 [October 1967]: 514–15); and Fred Steiner, "Herrmann's 'Black-and-White' Music for Hitchcock's *Psycho*," *Film Music Notebook* 1, no. 1 (Fall 1974): 28–36 and 1, no. 2 (Winter 1974–1975): 26–46.

11. *Citizen Kane* Manuscript Score, Music Section, Library of Congress. (ML96H4717CASE)

12. Dave Dreyer to Harold Hendee, May 18, 1940.

13. Bruce, *Bernard Herrmann*, provides a detailed analysis of how these two musical motifs function as elements of narration.

14. The question of the opera's provenance was part of the Mankiewicz–Welles scripting controversy (see Atkins for a summary). My source for the information given here is the RKO *Citizen Kane* Music File. On June 11, 1940, the RKO Music Department asked the New York office to secure the rights to the mirror scene from *Thaïs* for Welles's use. A clarification of June 13 explained that it was to be used "against action in theatre audience." In a letter of July 8, New York advised that there had been no reply to an inquiry and recommended that a substitution be considered (Correspondence, Dreyer and Hendee). Welles's wire to Herrmann was first published by Bogdanovich in "The Kane Mutiny" and is reprinted in Atkins.

15. Herrmann, "The Contemporary Use of Music," 6.

16. Quoted in Gilling, "The Colour of the Music," 38.

17. Herrmann in Cameron, ed., *Sound and the Cinema*, 121.

18. Interview with Robert Wise, July 18, 1978.

19. Herrmann, quoted in Gilling, "[On] *The 'Citizen Kane' Book*," 72.

20. "Bogeyman Makes a Movie," *Stage,* December 1940, 54–55.

21. *Hollywood Reporter,* January 3, 1941, 2.

22. Welles to Hopper, telegram, January 3, 1941, Hedda Hopper Collection, Margaret Herrick Library, Academy of Motion Picture Arts and Sciences.

23. *Hollywood Reporter,* December 30, 1940, 2.

24. "Orson Delivers," *Friday,* January 17, 1941, 24–26.

25. Stewart, "Development of Sound Technique," 229–31.

26. RKO secretary's note, January 9, 1941.

27. *Daily Variety,* January 10, 1941, 1.

28. Whether and to what degree Hearst was directly involved in the *Citizen Kane* affair has not been established. Charles Higham is doing research in the Hearst archives and promises to address the issue in his forthcoming biography of Welles.

29. Schaefer's version of the Hearst matter is given in Kael, "Raising Kane," reprinted in *The "Citizen Kane" Book,* 5–7.

30. *Newsweek* reported in its September 16, 1940, issue that the *Citizen Kane* script had been sent to Hearst and that he had "approved it without comment" (p. 12). This claim seems to me suspect. It can probably be traced to an incident involving Herman Mankiewicz. Mankiewicz brought up the Hearst matter with screenwriter Charles Lederer, nephew of Marion Davies, and gave him his copy of the script thinking that Lederer would show it to Davies. Lederer says he read the script but emphatically denies passing it on to either Davies or Hearst (Kael, "Raising Kane," reprinted in *The "Citizen Kane" Book,* 64; Bogdanovich, "The Kane Mutiny," 105). When Lederer returned the script, Mankiewicz somehow got the impression that the annotations drawing parallels with Hearst had originated in Hearst's camp and put out this word. A three-by-five-inch card appended to a photocopy of this script in the Theatre Arts Library at UCLA gives the story as it has passed down through the Mankiewicz family: "Marginal notes are those of the attorneys for William Randolph Hearst as they contemplated a lawsuit." It would have made no sense for either RKO or Welles to try to sound out Hearst at this late date, but it was in character for Mankiewicz: His widow told me that, after a producer expressed a strong interest in his controversial Aimee Semple McPherson script, he sent it to her heirs, but he was forced to abandon it because of their opposition (interview, January 6, 1976).

31. Interview with Robert Wise, November 14, 1983.

32. Kael, "Raising Kane," reprinted in *The "Citizen Kane" Book,* 41.

33. Esther Helm to Schaefer, February 13, 1941.

34. *Citizen Kane* Film Editorial Matters File.

35. Interview with Robert Wise, November 14, 1983.

36. For a running account of events, see the weekly stories in *Variety* for several months in 1941: "RKO, Despite Hearst's Ire, Announces Huge National Campaign for 'Kane'," January 22, pp. 3, 63; "Welles East to Talk 'Citizen Kane' Future," January 29, p. 2; "Welles, As 25% Owner of 'Kane,' Would 'Force' RKO to Release Pic," February 5, pp. 4, 18; "Decide Future of Welles' Pic by This Week," February 12, p. 4; "Hearst Opens Blast on RKO–Schaefer; 'Citizen Kane' Release Still Indef," February 19, pp. 2, 18; "'Citizen Kane' Release Date Not Yet Set," February 26, p. 5; "Luce's Time–Life Steamup by Welles to Force 'Citizen Kane' Release; $800,000 Prod. Now May Be Stalled," March 5, pp. 3, 63; "Welles Suing RKO on 'Citizen Kane' in Effort to Force Pic's Release," March 12, p. 6; "Welles' Threat to Raise 'Kane' Puts Him in Spot Between Odlum–Schaefer," March 19, p. 7; "N. Y. Legiter to House 'Citizen Kane' Day-and-Date with RKO Palace, B'way," April 9, p. 6; "Hearst Papers' Anti-'Citizen Kane' Gripe Takes It Out on Welles–CBS," April 16, pp. 3, 52; "Add: Hearst vs. Welles ('Citizen Kane'); More Newspaper Attacks," April 23, p. 7; "RKO's Watchful Waiting on Hearst Papers' Further Reaction to 'Kane'," May 7, p. 6. Also see Douglas W. Churchill, "Orson Welles Scares Hollywood," *New York Times,* January 19, 1941, IX: 5; "Hearst vs. Orson Welles," *Newsweek,* January 20, 1941,

62–63; "Citizen Welles Raises Kane," *Time,* January 27, 1941, 69–70; "Kane Case," *Time,* March 17, 1941, 90–92.

37. Stewart, "Development of Sound Technique," 231.

38. *Citizen Kane* Film Exhibition Matters File.

39. *Film Daily,* April 7, 1941, 1, 6.

40. *Variety,* May 14, 1941, 4.

41. Kael, "Raising Kane," reprinted in *The 'Citizen Kane' Book,* 41.

42. The review excerpts are from Genee Lesser [Fadiman], *Columbus* [Ohio] *Citizen,* April 6, 1941; Kate Cameron, *New York Daily-News,* May 2, 1941; William Boehnel, *New York World Telegram,* May 2, 1941; Otis Ferguson, *The New Republic,* June 2, 1941, reprinted in Gottesman, ed., *Focus on "Citizen Kane,"* 51; Philip T. Hartung, *The Commonweal,* May 9, 1941, 65.

43. See the weekly charts of picture grosses in *Variety,* May 7, 1941 –April 8, 1942, and the accompanying stories. Before the New York opening, the film played in Philadelphia and Pittsburgh in March to test the market.

44. "Welles and 'Kane' Doped to Win Flock of Oscars Next Week, But 'Valley' and 'York' (Cooper) Hot Faves Also," *Variety,* February 18, 1942, 4, 20; "Extras Scuttled Welles; Ad Splash Big Aid to 'Valley'" and "Orson Welles' Near-Washout Rated Biggest Upset in Academy Stakes; 'Valley,' Cooper, Fontaine, Ford Cop," *Variety,* March 4, 1942, 4.

45. Edward Connor, letter to the editor, *New York Times,* January 25, 1948, II: 4.

46. Richard Griffith, "The Film Since Then," in Paul Rotha, *The Film Till Now: A Survey of World Cinema,* rev. and enl. (London: Spring, 1967), 495–97.

47. Arthur Knight, *The Liveliest Art: A Panoramic History of the Movies* (New York: Macmillan, 1957), 186–89.

48. The French reception is summarized by Dudley Andrew in *André Bazin* (New York: Oxford University Press, 1978), 123–25. Andrew gives the impression that, except for the little magazines, reaction to the film in France was generally negative. This view has been challenged by Michel Ciment in *Positif,* November 1983, 76–77.

49. *La Revue du cinéma,* issues of December 1946, January 1947, February 1947, February 1948, March 1948, and October 1948. See the bibliography for a detailed listing of articles from these issues.

50. André Bazin, *Orson Welles,* preface by Jean Cocteau (Paris: Chavane, 1950), 52–55, translated in Gottesman, ed., *Focus on "Citizen Kane,"* 128–29.

51. André Bazin, *What Is Cinema?,* translated and edited by Hugh Gray (Berkeley: University of California Press, 1967), 37.

52. François Truffaut, *"Citizen Kane," L'Express* (November 26, 1959), translated in Gottesman, ed., *Focus on "Citizen Kane,"* 131.

53. Jean-Luc Godard, *"La Ligne de mire," Cahiers du cinéma* no. 93 (March 1959), translated in *Godard on Godard,* ed. Jean Narboni and Tom Milne (New York: Viking, 1972), 128.

54. Peter Bogdanovich, *The Cinema of Orson Welles* (New York: Film Library of the Museum of Modern Art, 1961), 3.

55. On the sale of the RKO library to television, see "RKO Radio Pictures Leases 740 Feature, Other Films for TV Use to C & C Super Corp. for $15 Million," *Wall Street Journal,* December 27, 1955.

56. Archer's essay on Elia Kazan in *Film Culture* 2, no. 2, issue 8 (1956): 5–7, 21–24 is a good example of American auteur criticism before the French influence was felt; it is a prototype of the kind of career surveys that flourished in the 1960s and 1970s.

57. Andrew Sarris, *"Citizen Kane:* The American Baroque," *Film Culture* 2, no. 3, issue 9 (1956): 14–16; reprinted in *Focus on "Citizen Kane,"* 102–8.

58. Andrew Sarris, *The American Cinema: Directors and Directions, 1929–1968* (New York: E. P. Dutton, 1968), 78.

59. Peter Cowie, *The Cinema of Orson Welles* (New York: A. S. Barnes, 1965).

60. "The Great American Films" (Los Angeles: Filmex, 1973), promotional flyer. Vernon Scott, "Top Movies Are Listed [in USC Poll]" (Hollywood: United Press International, November 26, 1972), wire service story. "The American Film Institute Survey," in Cobbett Steinberg, *Reel Facts: The Movie Book of Records* (New York: Vintage, 1982), 142-44; information on rankings provided to the author by the American Film Institute. *Citizen Kane* feature, "All Things Considered" (Washington, D.C.: National Public Radio, November 17, 1977), radio broadcast.

61. *National Survey of Film and Television Higher Education Report on Findings* (Washington, D.C.: American Film Institute, August 1976), pamphlet.

62. Robert L. Carringer, "Rosebud, Dead or Alive: Narrative and Symbolic Structure in *Citizen Kane*," *PMLA* 91, no. 2 (March 1976): 185-93.

63. The *Sight and Sound* lists through 1972 are given in Steinberg, 125-26. The history of the poll is summarized in "'Kane' Tops All-Time Best Pic Poll Yet Again: 30-Yr. Hold," *Variety*, December 1, 1982, 4, 22.

Notes to Chapter Six

1. Welles wanted to retitle the story "Lord Haw Haw," but the RKO legal department objected, because it referred to a real person. No other title was put forth; the project was designated "Orson Welles #4" in studio records and referred to simply as "Mexican Story." In the script itself, the character was called Mr. England. There are two main scripts: "Second Revised Continuity," February 16, 1941, 139 pp., and "Third Revised Continuity," March 25, 1941, 168 pp. Joseph Breen of the Production Code Office approved the Third Revised Continuity with minor exceptions but cautioned about possible difficulties for the story material in Latin American countries (March 26). For a detailed plot summary of the script, see Naremore, 32-38.

2. Welles-Rogell correspondence, February 16 to February 25, 1941.

3. Welles to Schaefer, March 3, 1941.

4. *Variety*, April 16, 1941, 1.

5. Breen to Armour, December 10, 1941.

6. Leda Bauer to Schaefer, April 8, 1941.

7. Memorandum to agreement, July 7, 1941, revised January 29, 1942. Welles protested the new conditions, but Schaefer insisted they were in line with their verbal agreement. Welles would not sign the contract until just before his departure for South America.

8. There were two drafts of the *Magnificent Ambersons* script: "Estimating Script," August 15, 1941, changes to October 2, 1941, 196 pp., prepared by Kent from Tarkington's novel according to Welles's instructions, and "Final," October 7, 1941, changes to October 15, 1941, 174 pp. (Mercury has Welles's master copy with annotations on shooting by Kent and another copy labeled "Rehearsing and Recording Script" in Kent's hand).

9. Schaefer to Welles, September 10, 1941.

10. Schaefer to Welles, December 3, 1941.

11. Schaefer to Armour, January 23, 1942.

12. Welles to Moss, February 6, 1942.

13. Schaefer to Welles, March 21, 1942.

14. Moss to Welles, March 23, 1942. Welles to Moss, March 25, 1942.

15. RKO records indicate that all outtakes from the longer versions were destroyed, as was the print Welles used in South America. The only record of the longer version known to survive is a cutting continuity of March 12, 1942, which indicates a length of fourteen reels, 11,858 feet, and a running time of one hundred thirty-one minutes, forty-five and one-third seconds; for a summary of its contents, see Higham, *The Films of Orson Welles*, 195-97. The preview records and the cable traffic with South America are in the RKO and Mercury files

(see in particular, in Mercury, a four-page letter from Wise to Welles, March 31, 1942, detailing the preview reactions). The account of how Wise recut the picture was related to me by Wise himself (interviews of August 18, 1978 and November 14, 1983); production records bear him out. Wise reshot the scenes in which George and Isabel discuss Eugene's letter. Besides the ending, Fleck also reshot the scene in which George and Fanny prevent Eugene from seeing Isabel on her deathbed. Moss reshot the scene with Fanny leaning on the unheated boiler. Schaefer ordered one scene to be eliminated (George looking at his father's picture before answering the door and turning Eugene away), two others to be restored (Eugene and Isabel in the arbor discussing whether she should tell George, Lucy in the drugstore asking for spirits of ammonia), and another one to be retained (Fanny revealing her financial plight to George).

16. See *Variety* national box office surveys, July 22, 1942, 10 and July 29, 1942, 11.

17. These statistics are based on a profit-and-loss chart on individual films in the RKO files printed in Jewell, "History of RKO Radio Pictures," 749-67.

18. Welles to Schaefer, April 15, 1942.

19. *Magnificent Ambersons* daily production reports.

20. *Variety,* January 21, 1942, 7.

21. Wise made the claim that Cortez was demoted in the interview with Nogueira, "Robert Wise at RKO," 44. When I checked with him to see if he had been misrepresented, he repeated it emphatically (interview of November 14, 1983). Welles himself was evasive to me about Cortez. The account in this paragraph is based on interviews with several persons who worked on the film. For Cortez's version of the story, see Higham, *Films of Orson Welles,* 48-52.

22. Stewart, "Development of Sound Technique," 236-37.

23. The relevant figures, with another major RKO release added for purposes of comparison, are:

	Set Construction	Total Picture Cost	Percent of Total
Gunga Din	$105,968.23	$1,909,669.28	5.55
The Hunchback of Notre Dame	243,838.25	1,826,125.68	13.35
Gone with the Wind	197,877.00	3,957,000.00	5.00
Citizen Kane	59,207.00	839,727.00	7.05
The Magnificent Ambersons	137,265.44	1,013,760.46	13.54

The RKO figures are from the RKO files. Those for *Gone with the Wind* are from Roland Flamini, *Scarlett, Rhett, and a Cast of Thousands* (New York: Macmillan, 1975), 314-16. The figures for *The Magnificent Ambersons* are based on the original, uncut version. The revised figures are $139,093.50, $1,117,924.25, and 12.44 percent.

24. Card 117, Pomona preview, March 17, 1942.

25. This is the order of these events in the three versions:

Screenplay	Long Version of film	Release Version of film
Isabel's death	Isabel's death	Isabel's death
Major's sun monologue	Major's sun monologue	Major's sun monologue
Fanny's financial ruin	Jack's leave-taking	Jack's leave-taking
George's visit to lawyer Bronson	George's comeuppance	Lucy's Vendonah story
Jack's leave-taking	Fanny's financial ruin	Fanny's financial ruin
George's comeuppance	George's visit to lawyer Bronson	George's visit to lawyer Bronson
Lucy's Vendonah story	Lucy's Vendonah story	George's comeuppance
Automobile accident	Automobile accident	Automobile accident

Bibliography

Archives

Citizen Kane Manuscript Score.
  Music Section, Library of Congress. ML96H4717CASE.
Citizen Kane Scripts Collection.
  Theater Arts Library, UCLA.
Hedda Hopper Collection.
  Margaret Herrick Library, Academy of Motion Picture Arts and Sciences.
John Houseman Collection.
  Special Collections Library, UCLA.
Lundberg v. *Welles et al.,* August 18, 1950 and continuation February 15, 1951. Transcripts.
  Civil 44–62, Southern District of New York. Federal Records Center, Bayonne, New
  Jersey.
Orson Welles Collection.
  Manuscripts Department, Lilly Library, Indiana University, Bloomington, Indiana.
  Cited as *Mercury.*
Orson Welles Collection.
  RKO Pictures, Los Angeles. Cited as *RKO.*
Orson Welles Collection.
  Wisconsin Center for Film and Theatre Research, Madison.

Interviews

Interviews by the author with Hilyard Brown (July 17, 1978), Linwood Dunn (July 11,
1978), Ralph Hoge (July 20, 1978), Amalia Kent (various interview dates), Sara
Mankiewicz (January 6, 1976), John Mansbridge (various interview dates), Maurice
Seiderman (various interview dates), Darrell Silvera (July 19, 1978 and March 30, 1983),
James G. Stewart (July 10, 1978), Paul Stewart (November 19, 1979), Orson Welles (various interview dates), Richard Wilson (various interview dates), Robert Wise (July 18, 1978
and November 14, 1983), and Maurice Zuberano (July 18, 1978).

Trade Publications

The Film Daily. July 5, 1939, through December 31, 1941.

The Hollywood Reporter. July 5, 1939, through December 31, 1941.
Variety. July 5, 1939, through August 5, 1942.

Unpublished Theses

Gambill, Norman Paul. "*Citizen Kane:* An Art Historical Analysis." Ph.D. thesis, Syracuse University, 1976.

Jewell, Richard B. "A History of RKO Radio Pictures, Incorporated, 1928–1942." Ph.D. thesis, University of Southern California, 1978.

Rea, Donald W. "A Critical-Historical Account of the Planning, Production, and Release of *Citizen Kane.*" Master's thesis, University of Southern California, 1966.

Wallace, Roger D. "Gregg Toland — His Contributions to Cinema." Ph.D. thesis, University of Michigan, 1976.

Miscellaneous

Citizen Kane feature. "All Things Considered." Washington, D.C.: National Public Radio, November 17, 1977. Radio broadcast.

"The Great American Films." Los Angeles: Filmex, 1973. Promotional flyer.

National Survey of Film and Television Education Report on Findings. Washington, D.C.: American Film Institute, August 1976. Pamphlet.

Palmer, Christopher. Liner notes. "*Citizen Kane:* The Classic Film Scores of Bernard Herrmann." New York: RCA Records ARL 1–0707, 1974.

Scott, Vernon. "Top Movies Are Listed [in USC Poll]." Hollywood: United Press International, March 26, 1972. Wire service story.

Souvenir program for *Citizen Kane.* See under Books: Kreuger, Miles, ed.

[Tallman, Robert]. Third Rehearsal Script, "March of Time." December 3, 1936. Time, Inc. archives.

Books

Anderson, William J. *The Architecture of the Renaissance in Italy.* 5th ed. London: Batsford, 1927.

Andrew, Dudley. *André Bazin.* New York: Oxford University Press, 1978.

Artistic Houses; Being a Series of Interior Views of a Number of the Most Beautiful and Celebrated Homes in the United States. 2 vols. in four. New York: D. Appleton, 1883–1884.

Atkins, Irene Kahn. *Source Music in Motion Pictures.* Rutherford, N.J.: Fairleigh Dickinson, 1983.

Barsacq, Leon. *Caligari's Cabinet and Other Grand Illusions: A History of Film Design.* Revised and edited by Elliott Stein, translated by Michael Bullock. Boston: Little, Brown, 1976. Originally published as *Le Décor de film* (Paris: Seghers, 1970).

Bazin, André. *Orson Welles.* Preface by Jean Cocteau. Paris: Chavane, 1950. Excerpt translated in Gottesman, ed., *Focus on "Citizen Kane,"* 128–29.

——— . *What Is Cinema?* Translated by Hugh Gray. 2 vols. Berkeley: University of California Press, 1967.

Blake, Nicholas [C. Day Lewis]. *The Smiler With the Knife.* London: Collins, 1939.

Bogdanovich, Peter. *The Cinema of Orson Welles*. New York: Film Library of the Museum of Modern Art, 1961.

Bruce, Graham. *Bernard Herrmann: Film Music and Film Narrative*. Ann Arbor: University Microfilms International, 1983.

Calder-Marshall, Alexander. *The Way to Santiago*. London: Jonathan Cape, 1940.

Cameron, Evan William, ed. *Sound and the Cinema: The Coming of Sound to American Film*. Pleasantville, N.Y.: Redgrave, 1980.

Carrick, Edward. *Designing for Films*. Rev. ed. London: Studio, 1949.

The "Citizen Kane" Book. Boston: Little, Brown, 1971. Softcover edition. New York: Bantam, 1974. Contains "Raising Kane" by Pauline Kael, the shooting script by Mankiewicz and Welles, and the cutting continuity. The Little, Brown edition is cited in this book.

Chase, Donald. *Filmmaking: The Collaborative Art*. Boston: Little, Brown, 1975. Includes interview with Linwood Dunn, 292–97.

Conrad, Joseph. *Heart of Darkness*. Edited by Robert Kimbrough. New York: W. W. Norton, 1963.

Cowie, Peter. *The Cinema of Orson Welles*. New York: A. S. Barnes, 1965.

Fielding, Raymond. *The Technique of Special Effects Cinematography*. 3d ed. New York: Hastings House, 1972.

Flamini, Roland. *Scarlett, Rhett, and a Cast of Thousands*. New York: MacMillan, 1975.

Fowler, Roy. *Orson Welles: A First Biography*. London: Pendulum, 1946. Excerpt reprinted in Gottesman, ed., *Focus on "Citizen Kane,"* 78–101.

France, Richard. *The Theatre of Orson Welles*. Lewisburg, Pa.: Bucknell University Press, 1977.

Fry, Ron, and Pamela Fourzon. *The Saga of Special Effects*. Englewood Cliffs, N.J.: Prentice-Hall, 1977.

Gottesman, Ronald, ed. *Focus on "Citizen Kane."* Englewood Cliffs, N.J.: Prentice-Hall, 1971.

Griffith, Richard. "The Film Since Then." In Paul Rotha, *The Film Till Now: A Survey of World Cinema*. Rev. and enl. ed. London: Spring, 1967.

Haver, Ronald. *David O. Selznick's Hollywood*. New York: Knopf, 1980.

Higham, Charles. *The Films of Orson Welles*. Berkeley: University of California Press, 1970.

Hirsch, Foster. *The Dark Side of the Screen*. South Brunswick, N.J.: A. S. Barnes, 1981.

Houseman, John. *Run-Through: A Memoir*. New York: Simon and Schuster, 1972.

Huxley, Aldous. *After Many a Summer Dies the Swan*. London: Chatto and Windus, 1939.

International Motion Picture Almanac, 1941–42. Terry Ramsaye, ed. New York: Quigley, 1942.

Jewell, Richard B., with Vernon Harbin. *The RKO Story*. New York: Arlington House, 1982.

Knight, Arthur. *The Liveliest Art: A Panoramic History of the Movies*. New York: Macmillan, 1957.

Kreuger, Miles, ed. *Souvenir Programs of Twelve Classic Movies, 1927–1941*. New York: Dover, 1977. *Citizen Kane* souvenir program reprinted, 217–36.

Lambert, Gavin. *On Cukor*. New York: Putnam, 1972.

Lundberg, Ferdinand. *Imperial Hearst*. New York: Equinox, 1936.

McBride, Joseph. *Orson Welles*. New York: Viking, 1972.

Meryman, Richard. *Mank: The Wit, World, and Life of Herman Mankiewicz*. New York: Morrow, 1978.

Naremore, James. *The Magic World of Orson Welles*. New York: Oxford University Press, 1978.

Older, Mrs. Fremont. *William Randolph Hearst, American*. New York: D. Appleton-Century, 1936.

Orlandello, John. *O'Neill on Film*. Rutherford, N.J.: Fairleigh Dickinson, 1982.

Rotha, Paul. *The Film Till Now: A Survey of World Cinema*. London: Vision, 1949; rpt. ed. with epilogue by Richard Griffith, London: Spring, 1967.

Sarris, Andrew. *The American Cinema: Directors and Directions, 1929–1968*. New York: E. P. Dutton, 1968.

Schatz, Thomas. *Hollywood Genres: Formulas, Filmmaking, and the Studio System*. New York: Random House, 1981.

Souto, H. Mario Raimondo. *Technique of the Motion Picture Camera*. 3d ed. New York: Hastings House, 1977.

Steinberg, Cobbett. *Reel Facts: The Movie Book of Records*. New York: Vintage, 1982.

Tarkington, Booth. *The Magnificent Ambersons*. Garden City, N.Y.: Doubleday, Page, 1918.

Articles

"The Acme-Dunn Optical Printer." *International Photographer,* March 1944, 18.

Archer, Eugene. "Elia Kazan: The Genesis of a Style." *Film Culture* 2, no. 2, issue 8 (1956): 5–7, 21–24.

Bartush, Jay. "*Citizen Kane:* The Music." *Film Reader* (Northwestern), no. 1 (1975): 50–54.

Blanchard, Walter. "Unseen Camera-Aces II: Linwood Dunn, A.S.C." *American Cinematographer* 24, no. 7 (July 1943): 254, 268, 270.

Boehnel, William. Review of *Citizen Kane. New York World Telegram,* May 2, 1941.

Bogdanovich, Peter. "The Kane Mutiny." *Esquire,* October 1972, 99–105, 180–90.

"Bogeyman Makes a Movie." *Stage,* December 1940, 54–55.

Brown, Royal S. "Herrmann, Hitchcock, and the Music of the Irrational." *Cinema Journal* 21, no. 2 (Spring 1982): 14–49.

Cameron, Evan William. "*Citizen Kane:* The Influence of Radio Drama on Cinematic Design." In Cameron, ed., *Sound and the Cinema,* 202–16.

Cameron, Kate. Review of *Citizen Kane. New York Daily News,* May 2, 1941.

Carringer, Robert L. "Orson Welles and Gregg Toland: Their Collaboration on *Citizen Kane*." *Critical Inquiry* 8, no. 4 (Summer 1982): 651–74.

———. "Rosebud, Dead or Alive: Narrative and Symbolic Structure in *Citizen Kane*." *PMLA* 91, no. 2 (March 1976): 185–93.

———. "The Scripts of *Citizen Kane*." *Critical Inquiry* 5, no. 2 (Winter 1978): 369–400.

Churchill, Douglas W. "Orson Welles Scares Hollywood." *New York Times,* January 19, 1941.

Ciment, Michel. Review of Dudley Andrew, *André Bazin* (Paris: L'Etoile, 1983). *Positif,* November 1983, 76–77.

"*Citizen Kane* Remembered." *Action!* 4, no. 3 (May–June 1969): 26–35. Interviews with John Houseman, Richard Wilson, William Alland, Ralph Hoge, Paul Stewart, Agnes Moorehead, Joseph Cotten, James Stewart, Robert Wise, and Mark Robson.

"Citizen Welles Raises Kane." *Time,* January 27, 1941, 69–70.

Cohen, Hubert. "The *Heart of Darkness* in *Citizen Kane*." *Cinema Journal* 12, no. 1 (Fall 1972): 11–25.

Connor, Edward. Letter to the editor. *New York Times,* January 25, 1948.

Cook, Page. "Bernard Herrmann." *Films in Review* 18, no. 7 (August–September 1967):

398–412. Also see letters on this article in *Films in Review* 18, no. 8 (October 1967): 514–15.

Dunn, Linwood. "The New Acme-Dunn Optical Printer." *Journal of the Society of Motion Picture Engineers* 42 (March 1944): 204–10.

——. "Optical Printer Handy Dandy." *International Photographer,* June 1938, 14, 16.

——. "Optical Printing and Technic." *Journal of the Society of Motion Picture Engineers* 26 (January 1936): 54–66.

——. "Optical Printing and Technique." *American Cinematographer* 14, no. 11 (March 1934): 444–46, 470–71.

——. "Tricks by Optical Printing." *American Cinematographer* 14, no. 12 (April 1934): 487, 496.

[Fadiman], Genee Lesser. Review of *Citizen Kane. Columbus* (Ohio) *Citizen,* April 6, 1941.

Farber, Stephen, and Marc Green. "Family Plots: Writing and the Mankiewicz Clan." *Film Comment* 20, no. 4 (July–August 1984): 68–77.

Ferguson, Otis. Review of *Citizen Kane. The New Republic,* June 2, 1941, 760–61. Reprinted in Gottesman, ed., *Focus on "Citizen Kane,"* 51–54.

Ferguson, Perry. "More Realism from 'Rationed' Sets?" *American Cinematographer* 23, no. 9 (September 1942): 390–91, 430.

Gambill, Norman. "Making Up Kane." *Film Comment* 14, no. 6 (November–December 1978): 42–48.

Gilling, Ted. "The Colour of the Music: An Interview with Bernard Herrmann." *Sight and Sound* 41, no. 1 (Winter 1971–72): 36–39.

——. "[Interview with George Coulouris and Bernard Herrmann on] *The "Citizen Kane" Book.*" *Sight and Sound* 41, no. 2 (Spring 1972): 71–73.

Godard, Jean-Luc. "*La Ligne de mire.*" Translated in *Godard on Godard,* ed. Jean Narboni and Tom Milne. New York: Viking, 1972, 127–28. Reprinted from *Cahiers du cinéma* no. 93 (March 1959).

Goldfarb, Phyllis. "Orson Welles's Use of Sound." *Take One* 3, no. 6 (July–August 1971): 10–11.

Goldsmith, L. T. "Rerecording Sound Motion Pictures." *The Technique of Motion Picture Production,* Society of Motion Picture Engineers, eds. New York: Interscience Publishers, 1944, 43–49.

"Gregg Toland." *Sequence,* no. 8 (Summer 1949): 67–76.

"Gregg Toland [Filmography]." *Film Comment* 8, no. 2 (Summer 1972): 56.

Hartung, Philip T. Review of *Citizen Kane. The Commonweal,* May 9, 1941, 65.

"Hearst at Home." *Fortune,* May 1931, 56–68, 130.

"Hearst vs. Orson Welles." *Newsweek,* January 20, 1941, 62–63.

Herrmann, Bernard. "Bernard Herrmann, Composer." In Cameron, ed., *Sound and the Cinema,* 117–35.

——. "The Contemporary Use of Music in Film: *Citizen Kane, Psycho, Fahrenheit 451.*" *University Film Study Center Newsletter* 7, no. 3 (February 1977): 5–10.

——. "Score for a Film." *New York Times,* May 25, 1941. Reprinted in Gottesman, ed., *Focus on "Citizen Kane,"* 69.

Kael, Pauline. "Raising Kane." *The New Yorker,* February 20, 1971, 43–89, and February 27, 1971, 44–81. Reprinted in *The "Citizen Kane" Book,* 1–84.

Kahle, Alexander. "Welles and the Cameraman." *International Photographer,* January 1941, 6–8.

Kalinak, Kathryn. "A Study in Collaboration: *The Magnificent Ambersons* of Orson Welles and Bernard Herrmann." *Quarterly Review of Film Studies* 6, no. 4 (Fall 1981): 459.

"Kane Case." *Time,* March 17, 1941, 90–92.

"'Kane' Tops All-Time Best Pic Poll Yet Again: 30-Yr. Hold." *Variety,* December 1, 1982, 4, 22.

Luhr, William, and Peter Lehman. "'Would You Mind Just Trying It': An Interview with Special Effects Artist Linwood Dunn, A.S.C." *Wide Angle* 1, no. 1 rev. and exp. (1979): 78–83.

McBride, Joseph. "Rough Sledding with Pauline Kael." *Film Heritage* 7, no. 1 (Fall 1971): 13–16, 32.

"Miscellany. [*Citizen Kane* Script to Hearst]." *Newsweek.* September 16, 1940, 12.

Mitchell, George. "A Great Cameraman." *Films in Review* 7, no. 10 (December 1956): 504–12.

Nogueira, Rui. "Robert Wise at RKO." *Focus on Film,* no. 12 (Winter 1972): 43–50.

Ogle, Patrick. "Technological and Aesthetic Influences upon the Development of Deep-Focus Cinematography in the United States." *Screen* 13, no. 1 (Spring 1972): 45–72.

"Orson Delivers." *Friday,* January 17, 1941, 24–26.

Orson Welles. Cahiers du cinéma special series, no. 12 (1982). Includes Michel Chion, "Orson Welles Speaking: Notes sur la voix chez Orson Welles," 88–93; Bernard Eisenschitz, "Welles et le projet *Heart of Darkness,*" 108–12; and "Fragments du storyboard de *Citizen Kane,*" 114–17.

"RKO Radio Pictures Leases 740 Feature, Other Films for TV Use to C & C Super Corp. for $15 Million." *Wall Street Journal,* December 27, 1955.

"R-K-O Trick Departments Consolidated." *American Cinematographer* 13, no. 6 (October 1932): 45.

Reese, Harry A. "Merlin of the Movies [Maurice Seiderman]." *Saturday Evening Post,* February 28, 1942, 22–23, 37.

La Revue du cinéma (Paris). n.s. 1, no. 3 (December 1946) contains "Scenario (extraits): *Citizen Kane,*" 3–9, "*The Magnificent Ambersons,*" 10–12; Roy Fowler, "Les débuts d'Orson Welles à Hollywood," 13–17; Jacques Bourgeois, "Le cinéma à la recherche du temps perdu," 18–37; Jacques Manuel, "Essai sur le style d'Orson Welles (*La Splendeur des Amberson*)," 55–60. 1, no. 4 (January 1947) contains Gregg Toland, "L'Opérateur de prise de vues," 16–24; Jean-Pierre Chartier, "Les 'films à la première personne' et l'illusion de réalité au cinéma," 32–41. 1, no. 5 (February 1947) contains Marc Soriano, "Cinq remarques sur Orson Welles à propos de *La splendeur des Ambersons,*" 54–57. 2, no. 10 (February 1948) contains André Bazin, "William Wyler, ou le janséniste de la mise en scène," 38–48. 2, no. 11 (March 1948) contains André Bazin, "William Wyler, ou le janséniste de la mise en scène [suite]," 53–63; Jacques Doniol-Valcroze, "Rita est morte, à l'aube, seule . . . (*The Lady From Shanghai*)," 69–73. 3, no. 18 (October 1948) contains "Debat sur le réalisme," pp. 19–56; Jacques Bourgeois, "Le sujet et l'expression au cinéma (à propos d'*Hamlet* et de *Macbeth*)," 57–62.

Rosenbaum, Jonathan. "The Voice and the Eye: A Commentary on the *Heart of Darkness* Script." *Film Comment* 8, no. 4 (November–December 1972): 27–32.

Sarris, Andrew. "*Citizen Kane*: The American Baroque." *Film Culture* 2, no. 3, issue 9 (1956): 14–16. Reprinted in *Focus on "Citizen Kane,"* 102–8.

Sersen, Fred M. "Special Photographic Effects." *Journal of the Society of Motion Picture Engineers* 40 (June 1943): 374–79.

Slocombe, Douglas. "The Work of Gregg Toland." *Sequence*, no. 8 (Summer 1949): 69–76.

"Special Effects at R.K.O." *International Photographer*, December 1940, 4.

Spiegel, Ellen. "Fred and Ginger Meet Van Nest Polglase." *The Velvet Light Trap*, no. 10 (Fall 1973): 17–22. Letter of reply by Maurice Zuberano in *The Velvet Light Trap*, no. 11 (Spring 1974): 47.

Stark, Samuel. "Robert Wise." *Films in Review* 14, no. 1 (January 1963): 5–22.

Steiner, Fred. "Herrmann's 'Black-and-White' Music for Hitchcock's *Psycho*." *Film Music Notebook* 1, no. 1 (Fall 1974): 28–36, and 1, no. 2 (Winter 1974–1975): 26–46.

Stewart, James G. "Development of Sound Technique." An American Film Institute/Louis B. Mayer Foundation Oral History. James G. Stewart interviewed by Irene Kahn Atkins, April 11–June 20, 1976. Glen Rock, N.J.: Microfilming Corporation of America, 1977. Microfiche.

——. "The Evolution of Cinematic Sound: A Personal Report." In Cameron, ed., *Sound and the Cinema*, 38–67.

Tibbetts, John. "*Citizen Kane* on the Drawing Board." *American Classic Screen* 2, no. 6 (July–August 1978): 32–39.

Toland, Gregg. "How I Broke the Rules in *Citizen Kane*." *Popular Photography*, June 1941, 55. Reprinted in Gottesman, ed., *Focus on "Citizen Kane*," 73–77.

——. "Realism for *Citizen Kane*." *American Cinematographer* 22, no. 2 (February 1941): 54–55, 80.

——. "Using Arcs for Lighting Monochrome." *American Cinematographer* 22, no. 12 (December 1941): 558–59, 588.

Truffaut, François. "*Citizen Kane*." Translated in Gottesman, ed., *Focus on "Citizen Kane*," 129–33. Reprinted from *L'Express*, November 26, 1959.

Walker, Vernon L. "Use of Miniatures in Process Backgrounds." *American Cinematographer* 15, no. 4. (August 1934): 154, 162.

Wallace, Roger D. "Through a Lens Deeply: Gregg Toland as a Creator of Psychological Nuances." *Film/Psychology Review* 4, no. 2 (Summer–Fall 1980): 283–95.

Welles, Orson. "Introductory Sequence to the Unproduced *Heart of Darkness*." *Film Comment* 8, no. 4 (November–December 1972): 24–26.

Wise, Robert. "As the Editor, You're the Audience." *Film Comment* 13, no. 2 (March–April 1977): 21.

——. "Dialogue on Film." *American Film* 1, no. 2 (November 1975): 33–48.

Wyler, William. Letter concerning Gregg Toland. *Sequence*, no. 8 (Summer 1949): 68–69.

Index